T0327839

How to Train Your Sewing Machine

First published in the United Kingdom in 2024
by Skittledog, an imprint of Thames & Hudson Ltd,
181A High Holborn, London WC1V 7QX

Project editor: Gaynor Sermon
Design: Masumi Briozzo
Production: Felicity Awdry
Photographer: Xavier Buendia
Models: Milo Larcombe and
Maria Ferrero Cuadrado

British Library Cataloguing-in-Publication Data
A catalogue record for this book is available from
the British Library

ISBN 978-1-83776-037-4

Printed and bound in China
by C&C Offset Printing Co., Ltd

MIX
Paper | Supporting
responsible forestry
FSC® C008047

Be the first to know about our new releases,
exclusive content and author events by visiting
skittledog.com
thamesandhudson.com
thamesandhudsonusa.com
thamesandhudson.com.au

How to Train Your Sewing Machine

Rehana Begum
Illustrations by Akio Morishima

Skittledog

Contents

Introduction   7

Getting Started

Manual Machine   12
Digital Machine   14
Anatomy of the Machine   16
Threading   20
Useful Tools   26

Best Sewing Practice

The Handwheel   32
Starting to Sew   34
Tension   38
Needles   40
Threads   44
Maintenance   46

Essential Stitches & Feet

Changing Feet   50
Straight Stitch   52
Zigzag Stitch   54
Blind Hem   56
Buttonhole   60
Zipper Foot   64
Invisible Zipper Foot   68

Fabric & Patterns

Selvedge   74
Washing & Ironing   75
Grainline   76
Notches   78
Seam Allowances   79
Understanding Patterns   80
Fabric Cutting   82
Pinning   84

Practice Projects

Tote Bag   88
Hair Scrunchie   98
Lined Zip Pouch   102
Easy Gathered Waist Skirt   112
Envelope Cushion Cover   118
Apron   124

Resources   134

Introduction

How to Train Your Sewing Machine will teach you everything you need to know to begin using your machine with ease and confidence. It will demystify the complexities of sewing and introduce you to the basics necessary to get you started on this wonderful craft that is not only fun to do and yields practical, useful results, but can also be very beneficial for our environment, eliminating waste by encouraging repurposing and refurbishment.

With three decades of sewing experience and ten years of teaching dressmaking and sewing under my handmade belt, I want to share my knowledge and skills to help you learn, create and - most of all - enjoy using your sewing machine. Before we get into the nuts and bolts of the machine, let's first take a quick look at its story so far.

The sewing machine has a fascinating history, with several false starts. The Industrial Revolution that started in the 18th century required more efficient methods than manual sewing, and in 1830 Barthélemy Thimonnier, a French tailor, invented a machine that used a hooked needle and one thread, creating a chain stitch. But when tailors heard of his invention, they feared it would result in their unemployment and burnt down his factory - while he was still inside.

Four years later, Walter Hunt created America's first functioning sewing machine but did not patent it, anticipating that it would cause huge unemployment. In 1845, fellow American Elias Howe produced a machine which had a needle with an eye that went through the fabric to create a lockstitch. He struggled to market his design in the US, so tried his luck in England, only to return to find others had copied his lockstitch mechanism.

One of those was Isaac Merritt Singer, who in 1851 developed the first version of our modern sewing machine, with a foot pedal and the up-and-down needle. Elements from the Howe, Hunt and Thimonnier inventions 'inspired' Singer, causing Howe to file a lawsuit, which he won, and Singer was forced to give him a share of profits from his company.

So it's safe to say that sewing machines have been around for a long time and are here to stay, enjoying continued use as people discover or rediscover the fun of sewing. During the covid pandemic there was a rise in people buying sewing machines, with many stores reporting shortages. Evidently there was a need to get back to working with our hands and being creative, which aids relaxation and mindfulness, feels therapeutic and promotes slow fashion.

I may be biased, but every finished make or refreshed garment fills me with immense pride and joy. In today's economic climate, where the impact of waste from the fashion industry continues to threaten global environments and communities, focusing on our

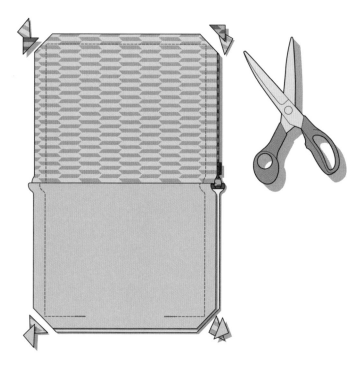

personal impact, as well as the community around us, is one way we can ensure our collective commitment to sustainability counts. Sewing is a great place to start.

When we have the ability to sew, we are able to alter, repair and upcycle, breathing new life into old things, saving them from the landfill while saving us money too. And by repurposing and upcycling our existing wardrobe and home accessories, we can help reduce local waste and unnecessary purchases, as well as spread awareness of the methods employed in clothing and furnishing production to encourage sustainable choices. Sewing can educate us on fabric quality, fit and the construction process, hopefully making us more conscious consumers.

There are many ways to give a new lease of life to our clothes, from adding pockets and trims to adjusting the length of hems and sleeves, as well as replacing buttons and zips or using patches. Increasing the longevity of our clothes, as well as championing quality over quantity, means we can reduce our carbon footprint as well as create opportunities for new sewing projects. Being able to sew gives us the opportunity to design and make unique garments and home accessories that suit and fit us better, making us more likely to want to keep them for longer.

This book will hopefully inspire you to do some, if not all, of the above. I will start by introducing the sewing machine and all of its important parts, then show you how to set it up and use the main features. You will discover how to troubleshoot machine problems, use a basic pattern, and select and work with different fabrics. Finally, you will find a selection of simple but satisfying projects so that you can put your new skills into practice straight away, and proudly say, 'I made this!'

Getting Started

Manual Machine

BOBBIN WIND
TENSION DISC

THREAD GUIDE

TAKE-UP LEVER

There are many different brands and models of sewing machines available. For beginner sewers this can be overwhelming, especially when choosing your first machine. However, while sewing machines can at first appear complicated and different from one machine to another, most have the same essential parts (albeit in different locations on the machine). Familiarizing yourself with the common parts of your machine will help you to operate it comfortably and efficiently.

On the following pages are the two most popular types of domestic sewing machine – a manual model and a digital model – each highlighting the essential parts for regular sewing.

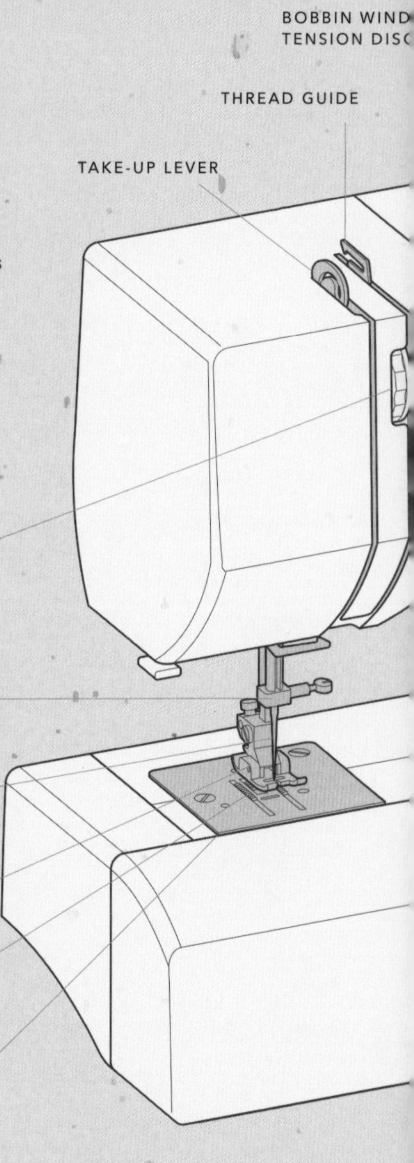

TENSION CONTROL

NEEDLE CLAMP

NEEDLE

PRESSER FOOT

FEED DOGS

NEEDLE PLATE

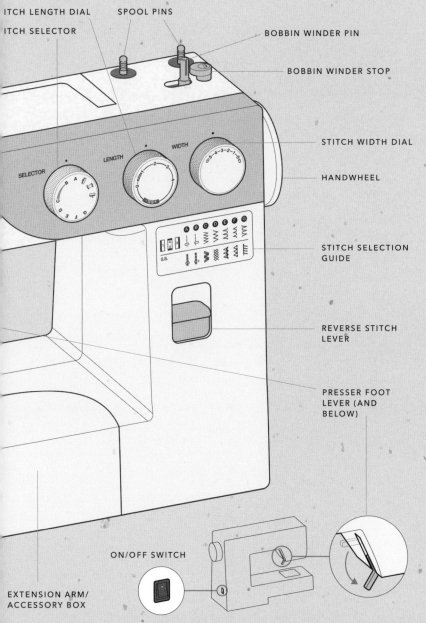

ITCH LENGTH DIAL

ITCH SELECTOR

SPOOL PINS

BOBBIN WINDER PIN

BOBBIN WINDER STOP

STITCH WIDTH DIAL

HANDWHEEL

STITCH SELECTION GUIDE

REVERSE STITCH LEVER

PRESSER FOOT LEVER (AND BELOW)

ON/OFF SWITCH

EXTENSION ARM/ ACCESSORY BOX

Digital Machine

BOBBIN WINDER
TENSION DISC

Digital machines include all of the controls that you'll find on a manual machine, but they also offer additional features that streamline sewing practice. One advantage of digital machines is the speed control dial, which is super helpful to beginners who may find achieving a consistent pace when sewing tricky. Another plus is, when winding thread onto the bobbin, the machine understands that it is in bobbin winding mode and so deactivates the needle from moving up and down (on a manual the needle needs to be manually deactivated before bobbin winding begins). The start/stop button allows you to sew without a foot pedal – not my preference but it's there as an option.

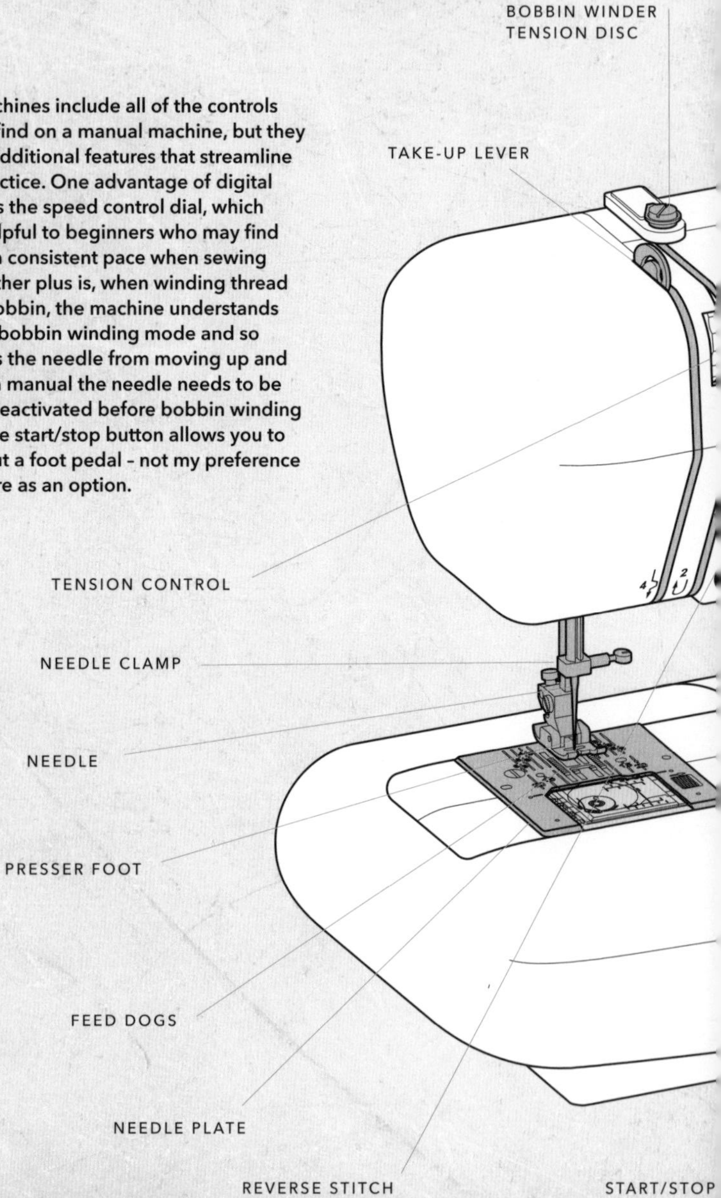

TAKE-UP LEVER

TENSION CONTROL

NEEDLE CLAMP

NEEDLE

PRESSER FOOT

FEED DOGS

NEEDLE PLATE

REVERSE STITCH

START/STOP

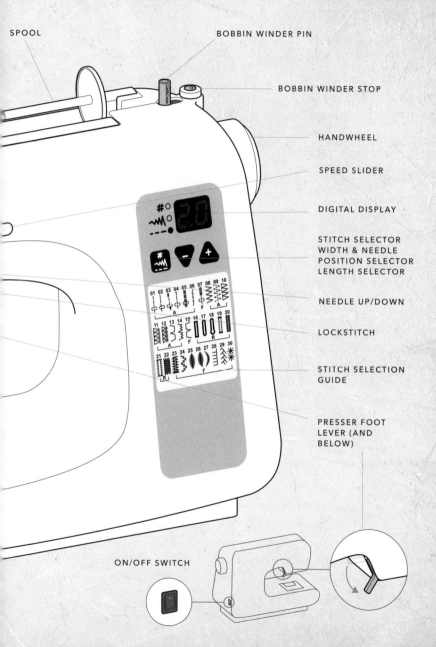

SPOOL

BOBBIN WINDER PIN

BOBBIN WINDER STOP

HANDWHEEL

SPEED SLIDER

DIGITAL DISPLAY

STITCH SELECTOR
WIDTH & NEEDLE
POSITION SELECTOR
LENGTH SELECTOR

NEEDLE UP/DOWN

LOCKSTITCH

STITCH SELECTION
GUIDE

PRESSER FOOT
LEVER (AND
BELOW)

ON/OFF SWITCH

Anatomy of the Machine

These are the basic parts found on most sewing machines. If you have a machine with different or additional features, always refer to your machine's manual. Once you know what and where everything is, it will make sewing a lot clearer and easier. It's just a matter of putting it all into practice.

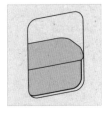

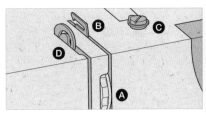

Reverse lever/button: On both mechanical and digital machines, this lever or button needs to be held down so the machine will backstitch (used to reinforce your stitching at the start and end of your sewing to stop the seams from opening).

Presser foot: This sits on top of the fabric to keep it flat while sewing. It is crucial this is down when sewing, or the machine goes a bit wild. There are lots of different styles of feet designed for specific tasks or materials, such as a zipper foot and a buttonhole foot.

A Tension control: This controls the looseness or tightness of the top thread so that it sews evenly and consistently with the lower thread. Tension needs to be adjusted depending on the fabric being sewn.

B Thread guide: Allows the upper thread to feed smoothly from the spool.

C Bobbin winder tension disc: When threading a bobbin it's important that the thread feeds smoothly and with consistent tension. Gently tug on the thread to ensure it is between the tension discs.

D Take-up lever: Usually a metal part that looks like a hook. You will see it moving up and down while you sew. It pulls the thread from the spool and feeds it to the machine. When threading, be sure to have the take-up lever at the highest position so it's in view, as the thread needs to catch through it and not drop behind it.

Stitch selection guide: Shows the menu of stitches and their corresponding number/letter on the dial. S.S. stands for stretch stitch, indicating stitches you would use on stretch fabric such as jersey.

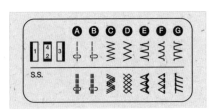

ANATOMY OF THE MACHINE

Remember

Always refer to your specific sewing machine manual to get the optimum information and use.

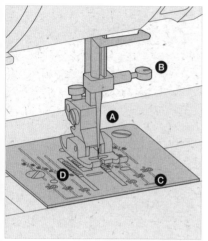

A Needle: Most needles have a flat back and this should be facing towards the back of the machine when inserted in place. It is usually threaded front to back when the eye of the needle is at the front. On some older machines the needle eye can be on the side, and should be threaded left to right.

B Needle clamp: A small screw that holds the needle in place.

C Needle plate: A flat, often square, metal piece located under the machine's needle and presser foot.

The needle goes through a small opening in the needle plate to draw up the bobbin thread from below. It often has guides on which you align your fabric edge in order to sew the correct seam allowance and sew straight.

D Feed dogs: These metal teeth work like a conveyor belt, which gently moves/feeds the fabric under the foot while sewing. It is important to always keep the teeth clean.

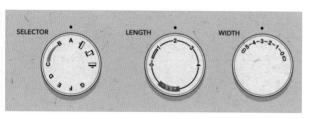

Stitch selector: Turn the dial (on a manual machine) or press the button (on a digital) to select the desired stitch. Most domestic sewing machines will offer at least the straight, zigzag, blind hem and buttonhole stitches as standard. Stitches offered can range from just five to more than 100 on some machines.

Stitch length dial: Turn this dial or press the button to increase or decrease the stitch length. The higher the number, the longer the stitch. If there is S.S. option on the length dial, when it is turned to this it allows you to access the stretch stitches. Often these stretch stitch lengths are fixed and cannot be changed.

Stitch width dial: Use to increase or decrease the stitch width; the higher the number, the wider the stitch. When your stitch has no width (i.e. straight stitch) then this dial refers to the needle position. Some cheaper machines don't include this dial and offer that particular stitch as just three different width options on the stitch selector.

Digital selectors: On a digital machine, you will often see the stitch, length and width selectors have a little circle that highlights the selected choice. You can then press plus or minus to access the range within: e.g. if you are on the stitch length and press plus, it will increase the stitch length, and minus will decrease it.

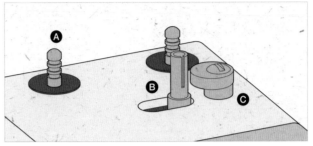

Ⓐ Spool pin/s: Rest your thread spool on the built-in pin to allow the thread to feed smoothly. If it's a vertical pin, as shown above, then your spool thread should run towards the left from the back of the spool.

Ⓑ Bobbin winder pin: The empty bobbin is placed here to begin winding the bobbin with thread from the top spool.

Ⓒ Bobbin winder stop: When the bobbin has been completely wound it should automatically stop when the full bobbin on the winder pin touches the Stop.

Horizontal spool: If the pin is horizontal, the thread is usually coming from underneath, towards you when threading. Some spools pins are upright, in which case the thread runs from the back towards the left.

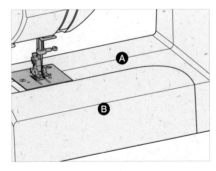

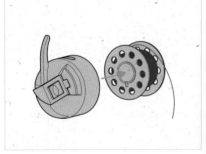

Ⓐ Workspace: The workspace is generally the amount of space located to the right of the needle. Longer arm machines mean more workspace, and a larger area to fit big items.

Ⓑ Extension arm: This provides you with a bigger workspace. Having a removable extension arm gives you the ability to do 'free arm' sewing, such as shirt cuffs, waistbands and trouser legs. It is also an accessory compartment, where the machine feet and other bits and bobs are stored.

Bobbin case: Front-loading machines have a metal case in which your bobbin needs to be placed before inserting it within the bobbin compartment. Top-loading bobbin systems do not have a case; it is simplified so that the bobbin goes directly in the compartment.

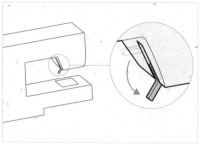

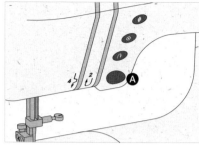

Presser foot lever:
This brings the presser foot up and down. Always lift before threading your machine as this allows the tension discs to remain open so the upper thread slips in between the discs.

A Stop/start button:
Can be used instead of the foot control/pedal. It will sew when you press to start it and stop when you press it again. I personally find it odd to sew using this feature and much prefer sewing the more traditional way using the foot control.

Foot control/pedal:
This is on a lead and needs to be inserted into the machine, usually on the left side of the machine. The pedal part should be placed on the floor. The pedal needs to be pressed with your foot to sew. How much pressure you apply will control the pace of your sewing. The harder you press the pedal, the faster it will sew.

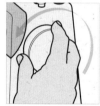

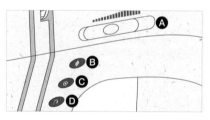

Power switch: For safety, the power should always be turned off when threading your machine or when cleaning it. If you do have it on (which can be useful if you require the light of the machine in order to thread the needle), then move the foot pedal away from you to avoid any accidents when threading the machine.

Handwheel: This is the large round dial on the right of the machine. It is connected to the take-up lever and needle and moves in rotation with both of these parts; simply turning the handwheel towards you makes the needle go up and down.

A Speed control: Usually found on digital sewing machines, this will control the pace of your sewing so that even if you press hard on the foot pedal, it will sew slowly if that's what you have selected as your speed setting.

B Up/down button:
Essentially the digital version of the handwheel. If you press once, the needle goes down; press again and the needle goes back up.

C Lockstitch: When you press this, it will do multiple stitches in the same spot without moving the fabric, like a full stop.

D Digital reverse button: You need to hold this down while using it, along with pressing the foot pedal, in order for it to backstitch. Release the button when you want to stop backstitching.

Threading

The most crucial step in learning to sew is knowing how to set up your sewing machine accurately. At first it might feel daunting, but once you've practised a few times it becomes second nature and can be done in seconds.

These are simple steps for threading a generic sewing machine: the exact method can vary from machine to machine, but most are threaded in a similar way. Refer to your particular sewing machine manual if you need more specific instructions.

Threading can be broken down into four parts:
• Winding the bobbin
• Threading the top part of the machine
• Putting the bobbin in its compartment
• The top thread bringing up the bobbin thread

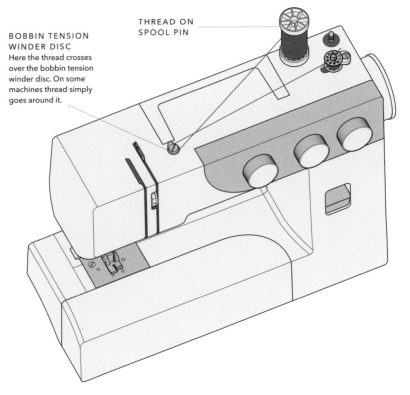

THREAD ON
SPOOL PIN

BOBBIN TENSION
WINDER DISC
Here the thread crosses over the bobbin tension winder disc. On some machines thread simply goes around it.

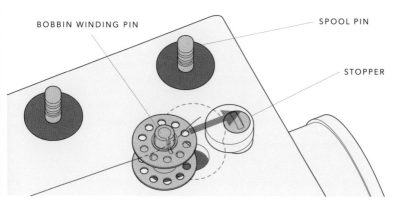

BOBBIN WINDING PIN

SPOOL PIN

STOPPER

Winding the bobbin

1. First place the thread spool on the spool pin located on the top of the machine. Some spools are vertical (the thread runs from behind) while others are horizontal (the thread runs from underneath).

2. Pull the thread end through the necessary guides – indicated on the machine with numbers or arrows – and then pass it through the hole of the empty bobbin (from the inside and out of the top).

3. Place the bobbin onto the bobbin winding pin. Hold the end of the thread and push the bobbin pin towards the stopper.

4. Depending on your sewing machine, you may have to deactivate the needle so that it does not move up and down when you start winding your bobbin up. On a mechanical machine you either need to pull the handwheel outwards or twist it loose to deactivate the needle. On digital machines the needle automatically deactivates when the bobbin pin is pushed towards its stopper, so you do not need to do anything.

5. Continue to hold the thread end and press on the foot pedal to start winding the spool thread onto the bobbin. After about 10 seconds, pause to cut off the loose thread end then continue winding up the bobbin by pressing the foot pedal again.

6. The bobbin should stop automatically when it is full (the full bobbin will touch the stopper, which creates resistance and stops the bobbin winding). Sometimes this may not happen – in which case stop when the bobbin reaches about 1mm (or about 1/32 in) from the outer edge of the bobbin. (If the bobbin is overfull it will not fit in its compartment; you can cut it so that it becomes a separate spool from the main thread spool.)

Threading the top of the machine

1. Take the top spool thread end (it is still on the spool holder) and pass it through the thread guide as indicated on your machine with either arrows or numbers. It will pass around the tension control and the take-up lever before going through the eye of the needle.

2. On some machines the eye of the needle is front facing and on others it is sideways. If it's frontal, thread from front to back, and if the hole is sideways, thread left to right. Some machines (often the more expensive) have a needle threader to help you. You can also use a separate needle threader tool if you find it difficult by eye alone.

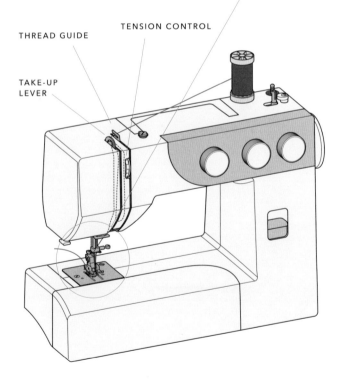

TENSION CONTROL

THREAD GUIDE

TAKE-UP
LEVER

Putting in the bobbin

Depending on the kind of sewing machine you have, you may or may not have a bobbin case that your bobbin goes into before being inserted into the bobbin compartment of your machine. Both options are demonstrated here.

Top-loading bobbins

Machines with top-loading systems usually do not have a case. This is a little easier as the bobbin goes directly into its allocated compartment.

1. Remove the bobbin cover plate by pushing the release button on the right.

2. Hold the bobbin with the thread hanging down the left side when held up in front of you.

3. Place the bobbin in its compartment and pull the end of the thread to slide into the marked groove, and then pull towards the left. Ensure the bobbin rotates counter clockwise. Don't place the cover back on until you have completed the final step, picking up the lower thread.

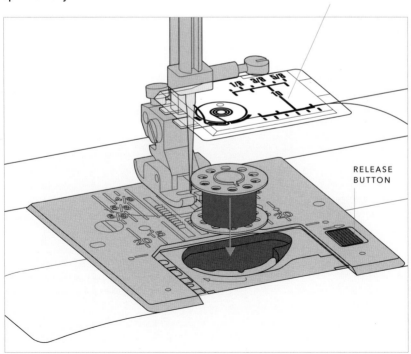

BOBBIN COVER
PLATE

RELEASE
BUTTON

Front-loading bobbins

1. Remove the front extension table and open up the hinged cover on the front of the machine.

2. Inside you will find a case; pull the tab to take this out. The bobbin needs to be placed in the case in a particular way: the thread must go in the direction of the slit found on the case and then be pulled over the hook.

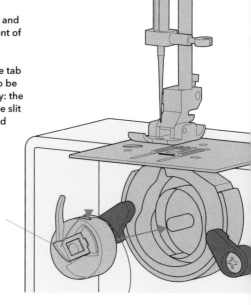

BOBBIN CASE

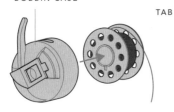

TAB

3. Place the case (now with the bobbin in it) back in the compartment, ensuring the hook point is sitting well in its allotted space. Turn it to the right until it clicks into place. Do not replace the cover until you have completed the next stage, picking up the lower thread.

BOBBIN LOOP

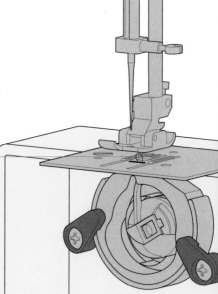

Picking up the lower thread

1. Hold the end of the top thread with your left hand. Always rotate the wheel towards you so that the needle goes down and comes back up again. Hold the top thread with your fingers while the handwheel is being turned to pick up the lower thread.

2. Keep an eye on the take-up lever, which you will see move down and rise back up to its initial top position. This lets you know when one cycle has been fully completed once. If you do multiple turns the thread can get tangled, so rather than watching the needle it is best to watch the take-up lever so you can properly see the completion of one rotation.

3. On digital machines, there is often an up and down button, in which case all you need to do is hold the top thread with your left hand and press that button twice. Look down at the needle and you will see a loop of the bobbin thread appear.

4. Gently pull the top thread upwards to bring up the bobbin thread, which you can then pull out and leave towards the back of the machine.

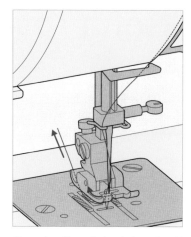

The top thread has picked up the lower thread loop, and now needs to be pulled up and out towards the back of the machine.

TAKE-UP LEVER

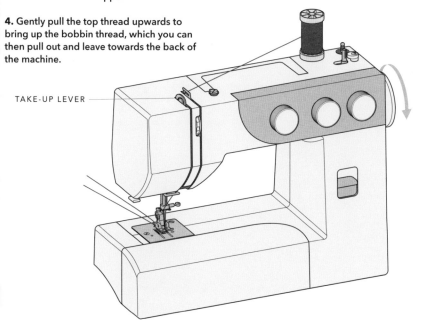

Useful Tools

FABRIC SCISSORS

PAPER SCISSORS

SEWING/
DRESSMAKING PINS

EMBROIDERY SCISSORS/
SMALL SNIPS

Fabric scissors
Good quality fabric/
dressmaking scissors
with a sharp end will
make the cutting process
easier and more fluid.
I like Fiskars 25cm
(10 in) shears, which are
dependable and good
value for money. Always
reserve your fabric
scissors for fabric only so
they stay nice and sharp.

Paper scissors
Use these for cutting
your paper patterns.

**Embroidery scissors/
small snips**
It's good to have a small
pair for cutting loose
ends and threads.

Unpicker/seam ripper
These are essential
for undoing mistakes/
stitches and unpicking
garments.

**Sewing/
dressmaking pins**
Invest in good-quality
pins that are nice and
pointy so they will go
through your fabric with
ease. Long, thin pins
are best. I use 34mm x
0.6mm pins. Beginner
sewers often prefer glass
ball head pins, as these
are easier to handle.

Pattern-making ruler
This is a dressmaking
technical ruler, which
is straight on one side
and curved around the
other. It is very useful
for adjusting/altering
patterns and for adding
seam allowances to
your patterns.

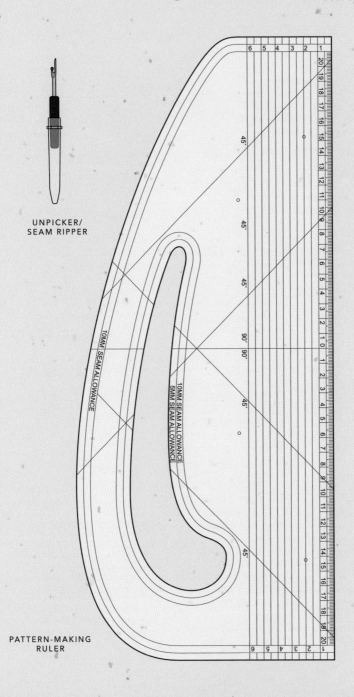

UNPICKER/
SEAM RIPPER

PATTERN-MAKING
RULER

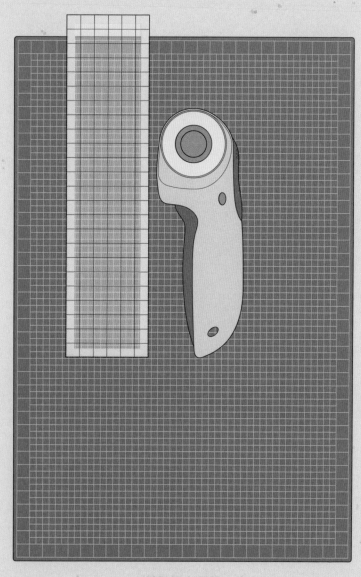

ROTARY CUTTER
WITH GUIDE AND
CUTTING MAT

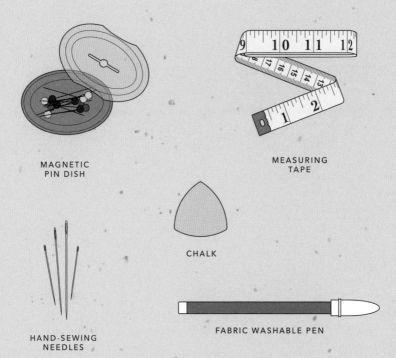

MAGNETIC
PIN DISH

MEASURING
TAPE

CHALK

HAND-SEWING
NEEDLES

FABRIC WASHABLE PEN

Magnetic pin dish
This is handy for keeping all your pins together and is also useful for picking up dropped pins quickly and easily.

Hand-sewing needles
Useful for finishing details, such as sewing on buttons and doing tailor tacks.

Measuring tape
Needed to measure the body, check and adapt patterns, and measure fabric lengths. It's good to have one with both centimetres and inches.

Chalk or fabric washable pen
Used to transfer markings onto your fabric. Chalk rubs off, and washable pen comes off with water or heat. It's always best to test on scrap fabric before use.

Rotary cutter with guide and cutting mat
Some people prefer to use rotary cutters rather than scissors. I find a rotary cutter useful for smaller accessory projects, and it is good for cutting out slippery fabrics like silk and jersey.

Additionally, you'll need to have an iron and ironing board handy. A good iron is important as it is used a lot in most sewing projects; ironing through the different stages of your make will result in a better finish.

Best Sewing Practice

The Handwheel

The handwheel controls the movement of the take-up lever and needle. The needle, take-up lever and handwheel all work together simultaneously. The wheel can be controlled by stepping on the foot pedal, or pressing the up/down or stop/start button on digital machines, or by hand on all machines.

The direction in which you turn the handwheel is very important, and it's worth stressing as it is a common error, particularly with beginners, to turn the wheel incorrectly. You should always turn it towards you (anticlockwise). Turning it in the opposite direction (away from you, clockwise) may damage your machine, especially if you do this often.

After turning the wheel to lift the needle, keep on turning it towards you to complete the cycle and see the take-up lever at its highest point; you will find this allows the thread to pull through with ease.

If you find you have a thread jam, you can turn the handwheel a small amount back and forth to help release the tension.

Turning the handwheel forward lifts the needle and brings the take-up lever to its highest point.

Troubleshooting tip

If the handwheel is not moving, you should first turn it towards you to see if it is locked. Sometimes the bobbin case is out of place, or there is something trapping the movement of the bobbin, which will not allow the handwheel to turn. If this is the case, this must be cleared/corrected before attempting to turn the wheel again.

The take-up lever should be at its highest point when you are threading and start to sew. When you finish sewing, make sure the needle is up and the lever is at the highest point before you pull out your fabric and cut your thread.

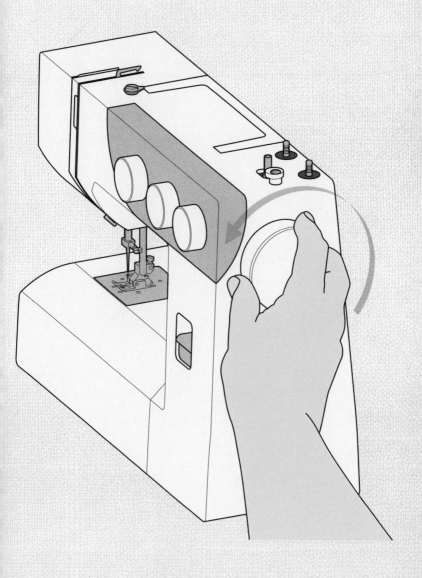

Starting to Sew

Once your machine is threaded and you are ready to start your sewing project, you should first do a test stitch on some scrap fabric. This allows you to check that you have threaded the machine properly and that the stitch setting/tension is correct for your chosen fabric.

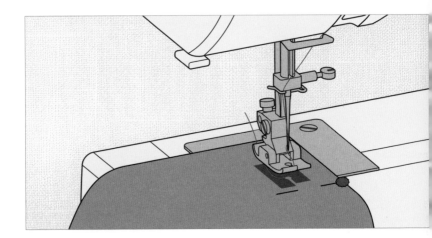

Beginning a stitch

1. Have your fabric ready and pinned (see pages 84–85 for pinning tips), and turn your machine on.

2. Set your machine to your required stitch, length and width/needle position. Often the first stitch on the machine is the straight stitch on a standard stitch length of 2.5.

3. Make sure the needle is at the highest point and the foot lever is up. Place your fabric under the foot and align the edge to the correct seam allowance guide on the needle plate (see page 79).

Needle is at its highest point and foot lever is up

4. Lower the presser foot onto the fabric. Lower the needle by manually rotating the handwheel towards you, or press the down button on a digital machine. Ensure both the top thread and bobbin thread are pulled towards the back of the machine.

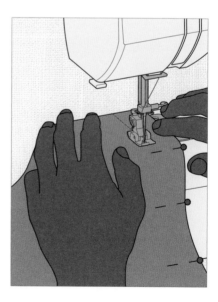

Presser foot and needle are lowered

5. If there is a pin at the start point, remove this now. I usually remove my pin after the presser foot is down so that when the pin is pulled out it does not drag the fabric out of position.

6. Position your fingers carefully to help guide the fabric once you begin to sew. Start stitching by gently pressing the foot pedal.

7. To reinforce your starting stitch so it doesn't unravel, sew down approximately 1cm (⅜ in) before reversing back to the top of the fabric - press down on the reverse lever/button while also pressing down on the foot pedal - and then go forward again to continue stitching.

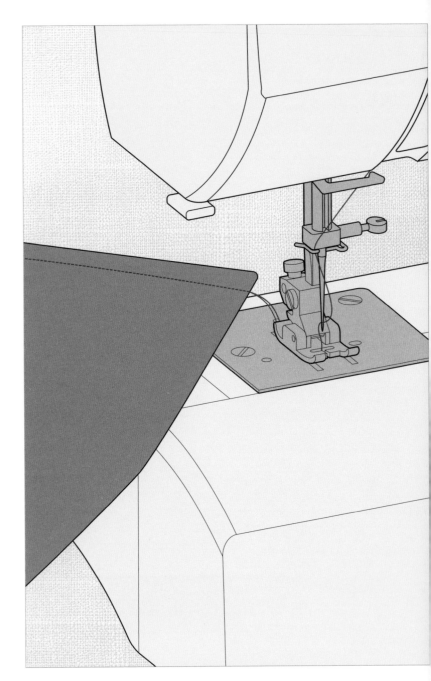

Ending a stitch

1. As you approach the end of your fabric, slow down a little so you don't overshoot the edge. You can even sew your last few stitches manually by turning your handwheel to have more control.

2. Make sure your needle is in the fabric a couple of millimetres from the end and then press the reverse lever/button and stitch approximately 1cm (⅜ in) backwards.

3. Now stitch forwards again to the end of your fabric (if you go a little off your fabric that's OK).

4. Make sure the take-up lever is at the highest point and your needle is up before lifting the foot up. Your fabric and threads should pull out of the machine with ease now, as you have completed your full stitch cycle. Pull your fabric out and leave a 10cm (4 in) strand of thread when you cut your thread away. This is so that, when you resume sewing, you do not lose your threading, which can sometimes happen if you cut your threads too short.

Take-up lever is at its highest point and needle is up

Why reverse/backstitch?

Reverse/backstitching is necessary whenever a seam will not have another seam intersecting it later. It secures the start and end of your stitching by backing up over stitches previously made, stopping it from unravelling over time.

Tension

Correct sewing machine tension is when the top and bottom threads are perfectly balanced; you shouldn't see any little loops on either the top or bottom of your fabric, and the stitching should look even on both sides.

Generally, the standard setting on a tension dial is 4. I recommend leaving it on this when starting a project and only adjust it if you notice your thread is looping or knotting, or the fabric is puckering.

If the tension is too loose, you may see visible loops on the topside of the fabric and the spool thread might be visible on the underside.

If the tension is too tight, the fabric can pucker, and the bobbin thread may be visible on the top side of the fabric.

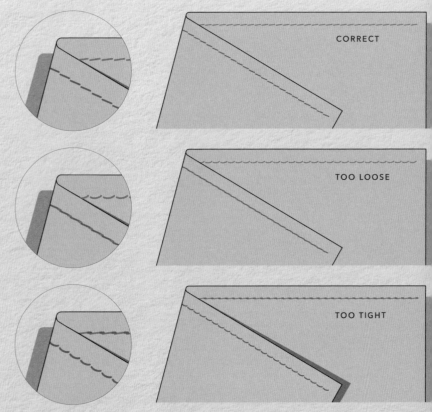

CORRECT

TOO LOOSE

TOO TIGHT

Adjusting the tension

It is useful to understand how the tension disc works so you can adjust it to the right setting for your fabric and thread. To create a row of stitches that looks the same on both sides of the fabric, an equal amount of thread needs to flow from the spool and the bobbin simultaneously.

When you thread your machine, the thread runs through certain tension devices. This includes tension discs, which squeeze the thread as it passes between them, while the tension control regulates the amount of pressure on the discs. When the tension control is adjusted to a higher number, the discs move closer together, increasing the amount of pressure (less space). Turned to a lower number, the discs move apart, decreasing the pressure (more space).

The type of fabric and thread you use also affects the tension. Using a thicker thread without resetting the dial will increase the pressure and cause the upper thread flow to decrease. When adjusting the upper thread tension, remember that higher numbers indicate tighter tension; this is usually better for finer, thinner fabrics. The lower numbers indicate looser tension, better for thicker, tougher fabrics. If you adjust the tension dial, always sew a few rows on scrap fabric before the real thing.

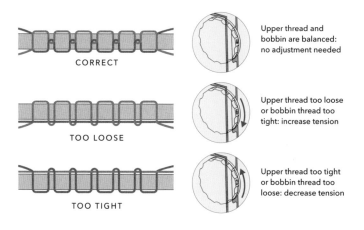

CORRECT

Upper thread and bobbin are balanced: no adjustment needed

TOO LOOSE

Upper thread too loose or bobbin thread too tight: increase tension

TOO TIGHT

Upper thread too tight or bobbin thread too loose: decrease tension

Check for other causes

Other factors can contribute to tension issues, so before you adjust the tension dial it is best to check if something else might be causing the issues. Often tension problems can be corrected without touching the tension settings.

- Is the machine incorrectly threaded?
- Is the bobbin filled correctly?
- Is the machine dirty – is there lint between the tension disc or in the bobbin compartment?
- Is any part of the machine damaged?
- Is the needle or take-up lever bent?

Needles

There are different types of needles for sewing various types of fabric, and using the correct type will result in a better-quality stitch. Understanding needles and their associated numbers will help you choose the best one for your fabric and thread, giving your projects a better finish. Using the wrong type or size of needle can cause them to break, create difficulties working with the selected fabric and result in poor stitch quality.

Anatomy of a needle

Learning to identify the different parts of a sewing machine needle allows you to understand just how they all differ, and how each one is tailored to suit a particular type of sewing.

Eye: the hole that the thread is put through. The eye size of different types of needles varies according to the intended thread type.

Shaft: this varies in thickness according to the intended fabric, with thicker materials requiring a stiffer shaft.

Shank: this is the upper part of the needle, which goes up into the machine and is screwed tight. The flat side should always face towards the back of the machine.

Point: the point shape varies greatly between different needle types, from a more rounded ball point for jersey fabrics to chisel-shaped for leather.

Scarf: this enables the hook to get close to the eye of the needle to avoid skipped stitches.

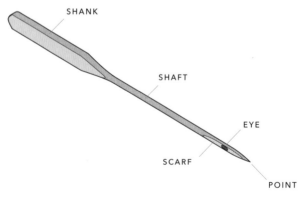

SHANK

SHAFT

EYE

SCARF

POINT

Understanding needle sizes

In addition to the different types of needles, they come in a variety of sizes. You will find needles sized with two numbers, for example 90/14: one is the European size, and one is the US size. From thinnest to thickest, the European sizes range from 60 to 120, and US sizes range from 8 to 20. Needles sizes are in relation to the diameter of the needle, for example an EU 90 needle is 0.9mm in diameter. The table below shows what size needle is best suited to the weight and type of fabrics.

US size	EU size	Fabric weight	Fabric type
8	60		
9	65	Very fine	Fine silk, chiffon, organza, voile, fine lace
10	70		
11	75	Lightweight	Cotton voile, silk, synthetics, spandex, lycra
12	80		
14	90	Medium-weight	Quilting fabrics, cotton, velvet, fine corduroy, linen, muslin, jersey, tricot, knits, light wool, sweatshirt fabric, fleece
16	100	Heavyweight	Denim, corduroy, canvas, leather
18	110	Very heavy	Heavy denim, heavy canvas, upholstery fabric, faux fur
20	120	Very, very heavy	Extra-heavy fabrics

Needle types

The following are some of the different types of needle available for a range of specific sewing requirements.

Universal needles: these are most common. When you purchase a sewing machine, this is the needle you will first find attached. A size 90 is the standard size – finer needles are mostly used for lightweight/delicate fabrics, and larger sizes are used on medium to heavyweight fabrics.

Ball point needles: these have a more rounded tip than a universal needle, which pushes the fabric fibres apart rather than cutting them. This makes ball point needles ideal for most knit fabrics.

Stretch needles: these are ball point needles that are coated to allow them to slip through difficult fabrics. They are used for sewing stretch fabrics and help prevent skipped stitches.

Sharps needles: these are designed to work with several layers of fabric thanks to a stronger shaft, which helps to avoid bent or broken needles.

Quilting needles: similar to sharps, these will sew through several layers of fabric and wadding due to their reinforced shaft. However, the needles are much shorter in length to allow quilters to achieve quick and even stitching.

Jeans needles: great for denim and densely woven fabrics such as heavy twill, canvas and heavy linens. Jeans needles have a very sharp point and a stronger shank to push through the heavy fabric and prevent them from bending or breaking.

Leather needles: for sewing real leather and suede (not imitation or synthetic leather).

Metafil needles: for metallic or rayon threads, these have an extra-large eye to allow the fancy threads to feed through more freely and ensure that they won't fray or split as a result of the sewing motion.

Embroidery needles: designed with a wider eye to allow threads such as rayon, polyester or cotton machine embroidery threads to pass through easily.

Topstitch needles: these have a large eye, which allows thick topstitching thread to be used. The extra-sharp point also allows the needle to pierce through all fabrics easily.

Twin and triple needles: used for pin-tucking and decorative stitches, and on jersey fabric as a finishing stitch.

Wing needles: used with special stitch options on your machine, wing needles will produce holes in the fabric to replicate drawn thread work.

Changing a sewing machine needle

How often you change a needle depends on how regularly you are sewing. Certainly, if you notice your needle is blunt, bent or broken, it will need to be replaced. Otherwise, changing it after roughly ten hours of sewing is advisable. Here are the basic instructions for changing a needle.

1. Turn your machine off.

2. Raise the needle to the highest point.

3. Loosen the needle screw by turning it anticlockwise (this can usually be done by hand, using a screwdriver, or you can use the little triangle provided in your accessory kit). The old needle will then drop down, but be careful that it does not drop under the needle plate.

4. Insert the new needle – the flat side of the shank should face towards the rear of the sewing machine.

5. Tighten the needle screw. It is important that the needle is up as far as it will go before tightening the needle screw, otherwise you risk the needle hitting the bobbin case, getting damaged and resulting in poor-quality stitching.

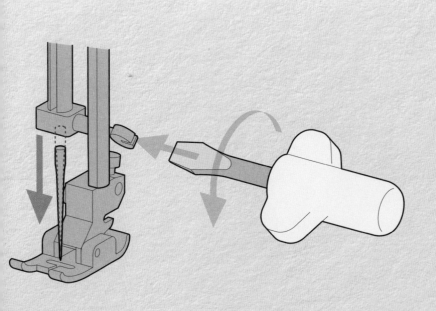

Threads

Just like using the right needle for your sewing, it is important to choose the right type of thread. Quality thread is smooth, should resist friction while sewing and should have enough give to keep it from breaking or making your seams pucker. Sewing thread also needs to be strong enough to hold your seams together against regular wear and tear and the rigours of washing.

There are many brands available, two of the most popular being Coats Moon and Gutermann. These are both established international brands known for their quality threads and wide range of colour options, and they offer a range of thread types from all-purpose threads to embroidery threads.

Stacked and cross-wound

The biggest difference between these brands is the way in which the thread is wound on the spool. Coats Moon threads are stacked (thread comes off the spool from the side), while Gutermann is cross-wound (thread comes off the spool from the top). All other brands vary between these two ways.

Stacked thread works best when the spool holder is vertical to the top of your machine. Cross-wound thread is better when the spool holder is horizontal to the top of your machine. Having said that, I often use Coats Moon on my horizontal spool machine, and as long as there are no nicks on the spool top, I've found it runs perfectly well.

STACKED

CROSS-WOUND

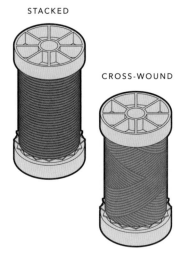

Different fibres

You can buy threads made from many different fibres: synthetic threads like polyester, nylon and rayon, and threads made from natural fibres such as cotton, wool, linen and silk.

The most widely used thread for sewing is polyester, an all-purpose thread that's strong and durable. Polyester thread doesn't shrink or fade when washed, and doesn't produce a lot of lint, which keeps the machine a bit cleaner.

Cotton thread is often used with fabrics made from cotton and linen, as they shrink in the same way. All-purpose thread can be used to sew these natural materials as well, but it's not recommended to use cotton thread for sewing synthetic fabrics. Note that cotton threads tend to be a bit thicker than polyester threads.

In addition, there are heavy-duty threads for sewing denim and upholstery or for topstitching, and more specialist threads for quilting and embroidery. Using the right thread for your machine and sewing project will result in smooth seams and stitches for a more professional finish.

Choosing threads

All-purpose thread	Made from polyester or a polycotton mix and known for its durability and versatility, the smooth texture allows for seamless stitching. This is the most popular multi-use sewing thread.
Cotton thread	Durable thread designed to be used with cotton fabrics and available in a wide range of weights and colours.
Silk thread	Ideal for machining delicate fabrics without snagging; also used for temporary tacking as it's easy to remove without leaving a trace. But this is a costly option, as silk threads are more expensive than other thread types.
Metallic thread	Designed for decorative stitching and embellishments; though delicate, its strength ensures durability and longevity. Requires a machine needle with a large eye to prevent breakage.
Tacking/basting thread	Soft cotton or polyester thread that's weaker than regular thread and used for temporary stitching as it's easy to break and remove.
Topstitch thread	Polyester or cotton thread that's thicker than regular sewing thread, used for visible stitching on the top surface of fabric and to reinforce seams and buttonholes.
Upholstery thread	Typically made from polyester or nylon, this withstands high tension and abrasion, perfect for stitching through thick fabrics like canvas and vinyl. Designed for heavy-duty sewing.
Invisible sewing thread	Often made of nylon or polyester, transparent and virtually undetectable. Fine texture and flexibility make it suitable for delicate fabrics.
Denim thread	Specifically designed for sewing denim; robust and durable to withstand heavy-duty stitching. Typically made of cotton or polyester and available in a range of denim colours.

Maintenance

Regular maintenance is essential to keep your machine running smoothly and efficiently. Treat your machine with care and clean it regularly to avoid issues. If you are sewing often, you should remove lint at least once a week. If you sew fluffy fabrics like wools, jersey and fleeces, the machine can get clogged up quickly, so it is a good idea to clean it immediately afterwards.

Cleaning

You should always consult your sewing machine manual for full details on how to clean your particular machine, but here are some simple steps that are appropriate for most machines.

1. First of all, always make sure your machine is unplugged before carrying out any cleaning and maintenance.

2. Usually, the main part of the machine that needs to be cleaned is the bobbin compartment. Remove the needle plate and bobbin to get under the bobbin case (you may need a small screwdriver to remove the plate screws, and this is usually provided with your sewing machine).

3. Brush out all the lint that has built up using a small stiff brush (found in most machines' basic accessory kit). Clean the bobbin area, feed dogs and hook. You can also brush around the tension discs and thread area. Tweezers are handy to clean out lint and stray threads.

4. Clean the exterior of your machine by wiping it over with a soft cloth. It is wise to protect your machine when it's not in use by covering it with a dust cover to prevent dust build-up on a day-to-day basis.

Note: It is important to use a dry brush for cleaning – you want to avoid moisture settling on your machine as this can cause problems with rust and your electrics.

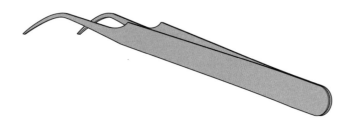

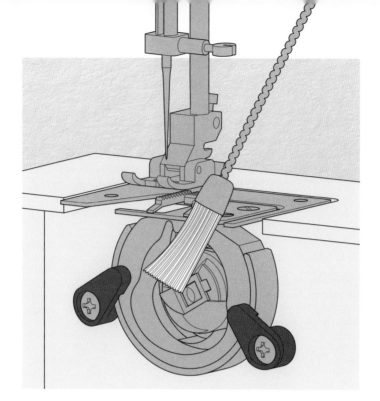

Oiling your machine

Many modern machines do not need oiling - consult your manual to find out whether yours does, and where to insert the oil if so. Generally, you need just a couple of drops of oil in a few different points on the machine.

• Common points to oil are around the bobbin case, near the needle clamp, and in the top of the machine (where there is usually a small hole).

• It is essential to use the correct oil for your sewing machine. This is important as each make of machine has an oil that suits its components best, and sometimes a small pipette of oil is provided with the machine. Sewing machine oil is often clear and fine.

• Always clean off any excess oil by test-driving your machine on scraps of fabric to clear out any residual oil that may spoil or dirty your real fabric.

• When your machine is well looked after, cleaned and oiled, it will perform much better, so make this part of your regular maintenance routine.

Essential Stitches & Feet

Changing Feet

When you buy a machine you will notice a few different feet in the accompanying bag of goodies. Usually these include a standard foot, zipper foot, buttonhole foot and blind hem foot. Using the correct foot allows you to sew with more ease and achieve a professional finish. You can invest in further feet aside from the standard ones, such as an embroidery foot and a walking foot. Knowing how to change your presser feet is important so that you don't damage your machine by attaching them incorrectly.

Three methods

There are a few different ways that feet are attached. You can have snap-on feet (which have a bar that clips onto the 'ankle' or stem), screw-on feet and full ankle/stem feet. Here, we provide a general step-by-step guide to changing the feet on your sewing machine, but if in doubt always consult your manual.

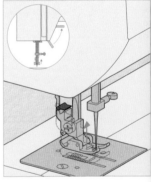

When changing any type of foot, first raise the needle to its highest position by turning the handwheel towards you so that there is a gap between the foot and the guide plate.

Snap-on foot (above and right)

1. Release the foot by raising the lever at the back of the holder. If it's a button, press it towards the front of the machine (do not pull it backwards).

2. Put your desired presser foot on the needle plate so that the bar on the presser foot is in line with the slot on the shank.

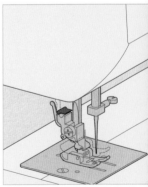

3. Lower the presser foot lever and fix the presser foot onto the shank. If the presser foot is in the correct place, the bar should snap in.

Screw-on foot

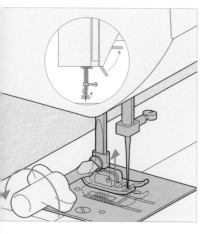

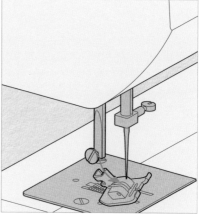

1. Release the foot by raising the lever. Unscrew the screw with a screwdriver or key. Once it's a little loose you can continue to unscrew with your fingers, then slide the foot off and out.

2. Slide the desired foot up along the side so the gap in the foot aligns with the screw.

3. Screw the foot tight, initially with your finger and then with the screwdriver.

Stem foot

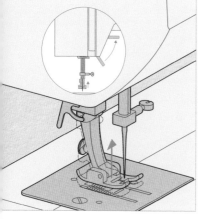

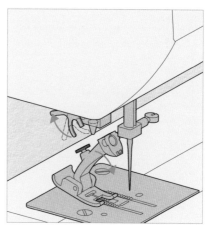

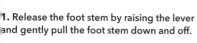

1. Release the foot stem by raising the lever and gently pull the foot stem down and off.

2. Slide the replacement foot up into the point as far as it will go.

3. Push the lever down so it hooks onto the top of the foot stem securing it.

Straight Stitch

The straight stitch is the most common, most used and most versatile stitch on the sewing machine. It is created when the needle (top thread) and bobbin (bottom thread) interlock when we press on the foot pedal/foot controller or turn the handwheel toward us.

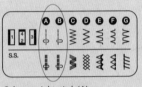

Select straight stitch (A) or off-centre straight stitch (B)

Selector dial set to A

Straight stitch presser foot

Stitch use

Straight stitch is used throughout construction in most sewing projects: to join fabrics together to create a seam, to do hemming, for topstitching and even for free-motion embroidery. One of the disadvantages of the straight stitch is that it has limited stretch, and is therefore not ideal when used on stretch fabrics. A longer straight stitch has a little more give, but is still not the best choice for stretch fabrics.

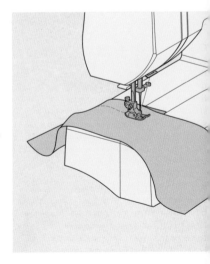

LENGTH

Use the length selection dial to choose stitch length. Below you can see examples of straight stitch across three different measures.

Standard chart showing stitch lengths and their best usage for particular fabrics, types of stitch and threads.

Stitch length chart

Fabric type	Length
Lightweight	1.5-2.0
Medium weight	2.0-3.0
Heavy	3.0-4.0
Leather and vinyl	3.0-4.0

Stitching type	Length
Basting	4.0-7.0
Top stitch	2.5-3.5
Gathering	4.0-5.0
Quilting	2.3-3.5
Stay stitching	2.3-3.5

Thread thickness	Length
Thin	2.3-3.5
Thick	3.0-4.0
Metallic	3.0-4.0
Rayon	3.0-4.0

Stitch length

One of the few adjustments you can make to a straight stitch is the length. The typical range is 0–4 but on some machines it can go up to 5 or 6. These digits shown on the machine usually correlate to mm. The standard length of a straight stitch for most sewing is 2–3, though I find 2.5 is best for general sewing. This range is common for construction sewing, machine quilting, edge stitching and understitching.

The 3–4 range is commonly used for topstitching, to create gathers or to sew a temporary stitch (basting), which will later be unpicked. You may opt for a shorter length stitch on lighter-weight fabrics, to sew darts and for corners and curves. Longer stitches can be used on medium or heavyweight fabric or when sewing through multiple layers. Short stitches are tighter and closer while longer stitches are looser.

Stitch position

The straight stitch is narrow and therefore there is no width option for this stitch. Instead, on some machines the width dial represents the needle position when on a straight stitch setting. Often, you will find that the machine needle plate has a series of guidelines (usually in millimetres and inches) for various widths of seam allowances when sewing with the needle in centre position (see page 79). If the needle is not in the centre position, the guidelines are no longer accurate, so the default is the needle in the centre when sewing construction seams.

Zigzag Stitch

The zigzag stitch is versatile and is probably the second most used after the straight stitch. When on the zigzag setting, the needle will move left to right to create the zigzag. On most machines the width and length are adjustable, while on some cheaper models you may be given just a few different widths. The behaviour of a zigzag stitch varies with different fabrics, which is why the width and length are adjustable.

Zigzag stitches displaying a range of widths and lengths

Numbers relate to the widths of the stitch and the space between zigzags, and can be made narrower/wider or tighter/more spread out

Stitch use

Zigzag is good for a quick-and-easy seam finish. It works well on all materials except for very lightweight or delicate fabrics and sheers. It emulates the look of an overlocked edge, saving the need for an overlocker as it can be done on most domestic sewing machines. Zigzag stitch can also be used to appliqué, make bar tacks and create satin stitching.

It is commonly used to sew stretchy materials like jersey fabrics and stretch wovens, as it's important to use a stitch that can stretch with the fabric. When sewing stretch fabrics, a narrow zigzag is best as it has just enough give to allow the fabric to retain its elasticity, while still looking pretty straight. You can also use zigzag to sew in elastics and for decorative purposes.

Stitch width

The stitch width usually goes from 0–5, and up to 7 on some machines. These numbers usually equate to millimetres, meaning 0 will remain as a straight stitch, therefore your button/dial must be at minimum on 0.5 or 1. The bigger the number, the wider the stitch. Some models only give two or three set zigzag options, a narrow, medium and wider one: these will do the job for most tasks.

Test your zigzag on a little bit of the fabric it is intended for because a selected zigzag width may look good on one type of fabric but not another. As a general rule, wider zigzags usually work best on thicker, sturdier fabrics and a narrower zigzag behaves better on finer, lighter fabrics. Tension is usually set to 4 for zigzag.

Stitch length

What you are using your zigzag for will dictate your chosen length. For example, if you are using it as a substitute overlock then you may want to keep the length spacing between 1.5 and 2.5 (any less and it can get too heavy and feel bulky for a seam finish, and if it's too long, the edge of the fabric may fray).

For some sewing techniques, especially for a zigzag where the length is short, it can be useful to use a satin stitch foot to help prevent the fabric from puckering, otherwise a regular sewing foot generally works just fine for this stitch.

How to use zigzag as an edge stitch

To use the zigzag as a substitute overlock, choose a width that isn't too narrow or too wide. If it's too narrow (under 3 wide) then it can be difficult to capture all the edge effectively. If it's too wide it can pull the fabric, making it look wobbly. Usually a width of 4-5 is best.

Once you have selected your zigzag setting, place your fabric under the foot: exactly where you place it is dependent on whether your needle is starting on the left or right of the machine. If it's on the left and if you've chosen a width of 5, then position the needle 5mm (³⁄₁₆ in) from the edge of the fabric so that when it starts to zigzag and the needle moves to the right, it falls over the raw edge of the fabric.

If the needle starts on the right, position it to start so it's on the edge of the fabric. When you find this, you will see where the edge of the fabric lies on the guide plate, then simply watch the edge of your fabric following this guide rather than the needle itself.

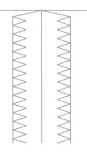

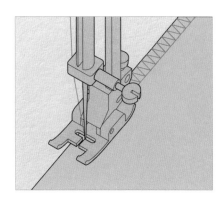

Blind Hem

A blind hem is exactly what its name indicates; a hem with stitches that you can barely see, essentially invisible. It's perfect for when you want a neat, discreet finished edge. Using a matching thread is best so that the tiny vertical stitches on the right side of the fabric can blend into the fabric. It's often used on straight hems on woollens and smart wear, and is a great hemming method for curtains.

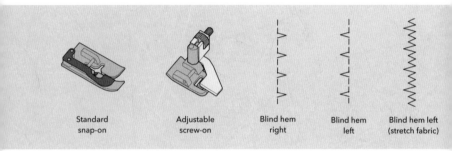

Standard snap-on

Adjustable screw-on

Blind hem right

Blind hem left

Blind hem left (stretch fabric)

To sew a blind hem, a blind hem foot is required. This is a special foot that comes as standard with most machines, although the look of the foot can vary from machine to machine. You also need to set your machine to the blind hem stitch. On a digital machine, once the blind hem stitch is chosen, the width and length will set itself.

If you have a manual machine, the instructions will state what width and length needs to be set within a given range. Either way, it is best to test on some scrap fabric first: if you don't catch your fabric in the correct place you will miss stitches, and if you catch too much then your hem will not lie flat.

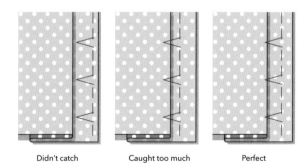

Didn't catch

Caught too much

Perfect

How the blind hem works

The majority of this stitch will sew on the seam allowance (see page 79) part of the hem and at every big triangle point of the stitch it will jump to the side to catch on the tip of the folded edge of the hem, creating tiny tacks on the right side. The stitches will look nearly invisible on the right side of your fabric.

The blind hem foot has a built-in guide called the flange, which rests against the folded edge of the fabric, allowing you to maintain a straight seam while you sew. It also ensures the space between the main stitches and the blind stitches are accurate. Most models include a screw on the side that lets you adjust the position of the guide.

Sew a simple blind hem

1. First you need to decide how big a seam allowance you need for the hem in order to get the required finished length. A blind hem works best on wider hems of over 3cm (1¼ in), so you may need to add a little extra seam allowance to your hem if it was originally designed for a narrower hem.

Say you have 5cm (2 in) of seam allowance to work with. Depending on your fabric, you will either need to fold twice for a light to medium weight fabric: 1.5cm (⅝ in) fold, then 3.5cm (1⅜ in) fold; or just once if your fabric is thick – it's best to overlock or zigzag the bottom edge and then fold your fabric up once at 5cm (2 in).

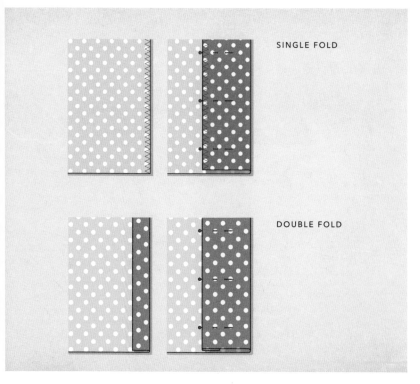

SINGLE FOLD

DOUBLE FOLD

2. Pin the fold in place with the tip of the pins facing down towards the bottom edge of the hem. Note that the illustration shows a double fold here.

3. Turn the hem back on itself. It should look like this. It should be wrong side up, showing a little bit (around 1cm (⅜ in) of the folded edge of the hem.

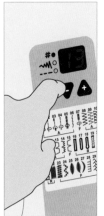

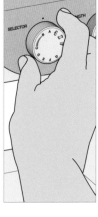

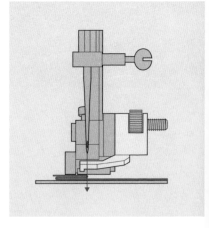

4. Make sure the blind hem foot is attached and the machine is set to make a blind hem stitch. Refer to your machine's manual to confirm the foot and the stitch number.

5. Slide your fabric under the blind hem foot and needle. The tip of the triangle of the stitch should be 1mm (1/32 in) from the tip of the folded edge (you will need to do a test stitch to confirm this).

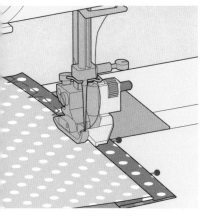

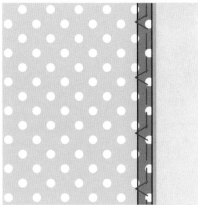

6. Adjust the flange to line up against the fold. As you sew, keep the folded edge right against the flange. As you approach a pin, pull it out with your free hand.

7. You will see the stitch is mostly stitching straight on the hem's edge that you left sticking out, while every few stitches there is a zigzag stitch. At every point of the triangle the needle reaches over and grabs that fold of fabric close to the edge.

8. Once you have completed the stitch, secure it with a couple of reverse stitches. Fold the bottom edge back down. It will look like this from the wrong side.

9. From the right side, you will see tiny tacks of thread that keep the hem in place, which are very discreet. Press well; this will help meld the stitches into the fabric, making them even more invisible.

Buttonhole

Machines vary in the buttonhole automation systems they have: some have a one-step buttonhole setting, while others may have a 4-6 step process. We'll show both here. Machine-made buttonholes are often created with two dense zigzag stitches (which makes a solid looking line/satin stitch) with the two ends reinforced with bar tacks. The stitch length on the parallel zigzags can be adjusted so the density of the stitch can be made heavier or lighter, based on the fabric you are sewing.

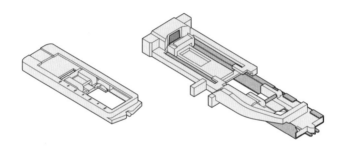

Button and buttonhole sizes

First decide what buttons you will be using to ensure you are sewing the right sized buttonholes. Buttons are sized according to their diameter, which is useful for helping to set your buttonhole stitch to the right size. Some buttonhole feet have a sliding gauge on the back where you can place your button so that it automatically sews the correct buttonhole size. Do a test buttonhole first to ensure you have made the right size, as sometimes buttons that are very low or very high in height may need to be made a little smaller or bigger, respectively, to take this into account.

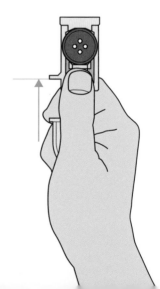

Buttonhole types explained

Standard
This is the most common type of buttonhole found on most sewing machines, and is created with two dense parallel zigzag rows (known as the 'beads') that are secured by bar tacks at both ends. This type of buttonhole is most suitable for medium to heavyweight fabrics.

Rounded edge
This is best for fine and delicate fabrics. The rounded edges are helpful in stopping/reducing tearing you may get with hard corners.

Keyhole
A more robust buttonhole used on medium to heavy fabrics and great for outerwear. The keyhole allows a thick button and thick layers to move through the buttonhole.

Stretch
As the name suggests, this buttonhole is the best choice for jersey and knit fabrics as the stitches are a bit less dense and slightly wider, allowing the fabric to retain its stretch.

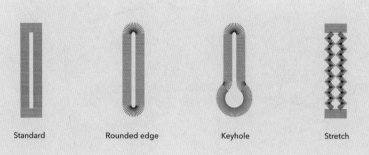

Standard   Rounded edge   Keyhole   Stretch

Buttonhole tips

Buttonholes are made up of dense parallel stitches, so it is a good idea to reinforce your fabric to stop it tearing. Use small pieces of fusible interfacing scraps for each buttonhole, or reinforce the whole strip where buttonholes will be sewn. Alternatively, use water-soluble stabilizer on both sides of the fabric to help the stability of the fabric while sewing your buttonhole; this can be torn away or washed out after.

Note this is a temporary stabilizer so it's still best to use some fusible interfacing or add another piece of fabric for added strength. Always sew a few test buttonholes on scrap first. This will help you line up your fabric properly to sew it in the correct place, and allow you to check that the buttonhole is the correct size. Buttonholes are stubborn to unpick if you get it wrong, so it's well worth doing a practice buttonhole or two.

One-step buttonhole

This type of buttonhole automation is very simple and doesn't require much work by the sewer.

Turn the stitch selector dial to select buttonhole, or on a digital machine press the digit for the buttonhole stitch.

Select the correct density for your buttonhole and fabric on the width selector dial.

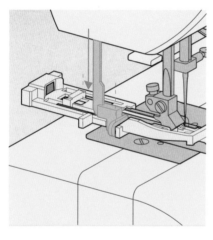

1. Place your button in the buttonhole foot gauge and attach the buttonhole foot to the machine. Often there is a lever positioned on the left side or behind the bracket on the buttonhole foot that you need to pull down (this ensures the machine stops moving when it reaches the length that is needed for the buttonhole).

2. Do a test stitch on scrap first to see where the stitch begins so you know which way the buttonhole sews, then you can mark a point on your real fabric. Most machines start at the bottom of the buttonhole and sew in reverse first. Position your fabric under the needle and press the buttonhole button to sew your one-step buttonhole.

Four-step buttonhole

This includes steps for manually sewing each side of the buttonhole. It will not require you to change any of the settings like length, width or direction, but you will need to change from one step to the next step manually (it usually indicates at which point you need to do the next step).

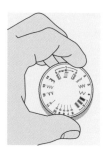

The 4–6 buttonhole dial will need to be turned manually after each step is completed.

1. Mark the size of the buttonhole on your fabric as shown. Attach the buttonhole foot to the machine and set it to the buttonhole stitch. If your machine has no gauge to measure the button for you, you need to mark it correctly on your fabric. Do a test stitch on scrap first to see where the stitch begins.

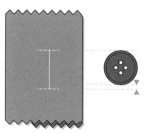

2. If you want to make a second buttonhole, reset your buttonhole stitch by changing it to something else before setting it back on the buttonhole stitch (if you don't do this it will just keep doing the last stitch in the buttonhole stitch cycle).

3. If you have no buttonhole setting, you can still sew buttonholes using the zigzag stitch. This option will require you to change the stitch length, width and direction manually after each step, so involves a little more work but is perfectly doable.

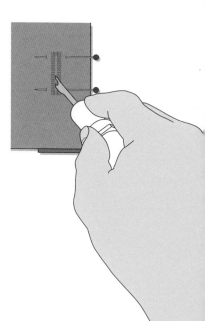

4. Open up your buttonhole with an unpicker/seam ripper, little embroidery scissors with a sharp tip or a buttonhole tool. Be careful not to overshoot your buttonhole bar tacks (you can place pins before the bar tacks so you don't overshoot cutting open your buttonhole).

Zipper Foot

For sewing in zips, there are feet available that make the process much easier. The zipper foot is narrower than the regular presser foot, enabling the needle to stitch close to the raised edge of the zip and puller comfortably. There are a few different zipper foot options, and they can vary from machine to machine but essentially all work in the same way.

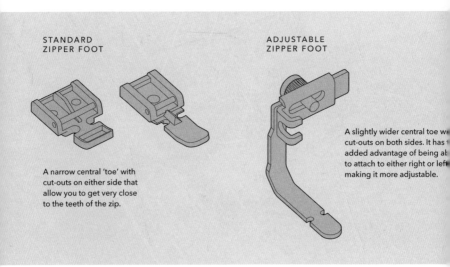

STANDARD ZIPPER FOOT

A narrow central 'toe' with cut-outs on either side that allow you to get very close to the teeth of the zip.

ADJUSTABLE ZIPPER FOOT

A slightly wider central toe w cut-outs on both sides. It has added advantage of being at to attach to either right or lef making it more adjustable.

The standard and adjustable feet can be used to sew zips in a variety of different ways, including a centred zip, lapped zip, exposed zip, open-ended zip and trouser fly zip. There is also an invisible zipper foot that is used to sew in a concealed/invisible zip (see page 68).

Sewing in zips is something every sewer will need to do when making clothing or home accessories. It can initially feel daunting to sew your first zip, but with the correct zipper foot and some clear instructions it can be easy and even fun.

Inserting a regular zip

Here we will show how to insert a centred regular zip with a standard zipper foot.

1. Overlock/zigzag the raw edges of the fabric you will sew your zip between.

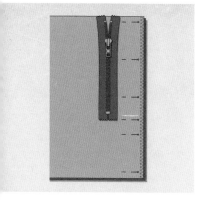

2. Pin fabric pieces with right sides together and place the zip on your garment with the top ends of the tape lined up with the top edge of your garment (or the top of the puller with the edge of the garment) and then make a mark on the fabric just below the stopper at the bottom of the zip.

3. Place your pinned fabric under the machine foot to sew a straight seam (here we have used a 1.5cm [⅝ in] seam allowance). Start with a basting stitch of 4-5 length up to the chalk mark on your fabric (this is a longer stitch as it will be unpicked once the zip is sewn in).

Once you get to the chalk mark, change your stitch length to 2.5. Sew down 1cm (⅜ in) before reversing back to the mark and then continue to stitch all the way down. Remember to backstitch again at the end. This 2.5 stitch will remain in your garment.

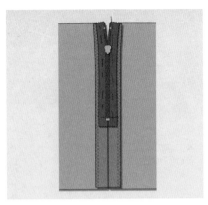
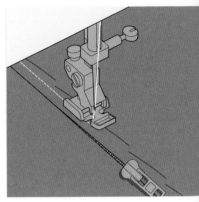

4. Press the seam allowances open, first on the wrong side and then on the right side. Pin your zip face down to the seam allowances and main fabric (all layers), making sure you line up the top of the tape to the edge of the garment and centre the teeth right on the seam line. Tack in place using a long running stitch and remove pins as you approach them. Put a pin just below the stopper at the bottom, and then on the right side of the garment mark a chalk line. Remove the pin.

5. 1.5cm (⅝ in) from the top, unpick an approximately 5cm (2 in) opening. Change your regular foot to a zipper foot. Attach to the bar on the left and position the outer left edge of the foot in line with the seam (the needle should be 5-7mm [¼ in] away from the seam). Make sure your zip puller is pulled down open. Sew straight down until you reach a little before the puller.

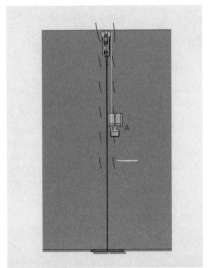

6. Keeping the needle in the fabric, lift up the zipper foot (A), which will then allow you to pull the zip up to the top. Put your zipper foot back down and continue sewing until you reach the chalk marking.

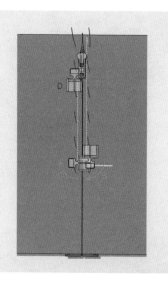

7. At the chalk mark (B), keep your needle down in the fabric and lift up the zipper foot; pivot to turn the fabric 90 degrees and sew a little bit past the seam (2-3 stitches on the other side of the seam) so it's an equal distance from the stitch on one side to the other. Often it is better to sew these few stitches by manually turning the handwheel.

At the next corner (C), with the needle down, pivot 90 degrees again and ensure the edge of the outer foot lines up with the seam and sew straight until you reach just before the puller (D). At the puller, keep the needle down, lift up the zipper foot and unzip the zip. Put the foot back down and sew to the end, remembering to backstitch at the end.

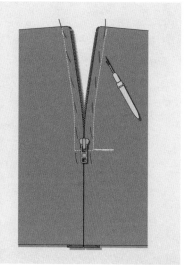

8. Unpick the seam all the way up to the top starting just inside the horizontal seam at the bottom of your zip. You can also unpick your initial hand basting running stitch too and you're done - one lovely, centred zip.

Invisible Zipper Foot

Invisible zips are sometimes known as concealed zips and are ideal for garments that require a clean, smooth finish, such as tops, dresses and trousers, and for household furnishings like cushions. They are intended to be discreet – there is no machine stitching visible from the right side as everything is sewn behind the scenes, hidden within the seam allowances.

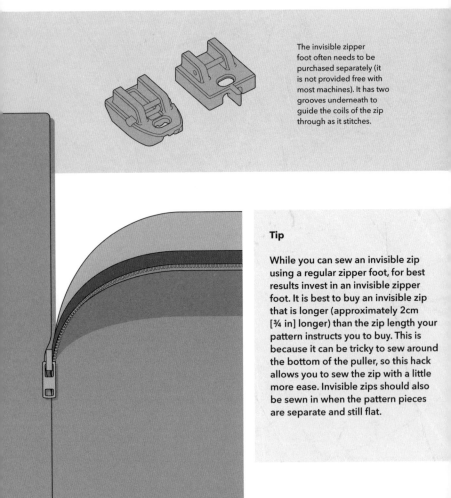

The invisible zipper foot often needs to be purchased separately (it is not provided free with most machines). It has two grooves underneath to guide the coils of the zip through as it stitches.

Tip

While you can sew an invisible zip using a regular zipper foot, for best results invest in an invisible zipper foot. It is best to buy an invisible zip that is longer (approximately 2cm [¾ in] longer) than the zip length your pattern instructs you to buy. This is because it can be tricky to sew around the bottom of the puller, so this hack allows you to sew the zip with a little more ease. Invisible zips should also be sewn in when the pattern pieces are separate and still flat.

How to insert an invisible zip

Here we will demonstrate how to insert an invisible/concealed zip using an invisible zipper foot.

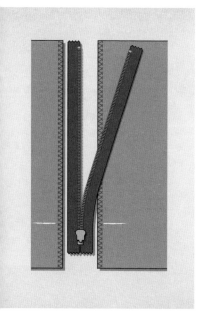

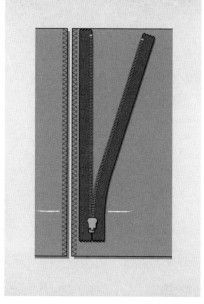

1. Overlock/zigzag the raw edges of the fabric where you will sew your invisible zip between. Measure about 5mm (³⁄₁₆ in) above the zip pull (while the zip is open) and notch and mark the measurement on both sides of the tape with chalk or fabric pencil (this is where you will sew up to). Transfer these marks to the edge of the fabric as well.

2. Place your garment right-side up and, holding your zip face down, place the right side of the zip tape facing down on the right side of your garment. Depending on your seam allowance, place the tape of the zip parallel to the edge of the fabric (here it is 5mm [³⁄₁₆ in] away from the fabric edge as the seam allowance will be 1.5cm [⁵⁄₈ in] and the zip tape is only 1cm [³⁄₈ in] wide). Make sure you line up the top of the zip with the top of the fabric if the seam allowance is the same, otherwise align the top of the pull with the edge of the fabric top.

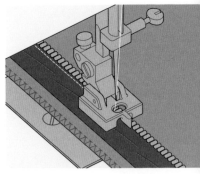

3. Baste in place, removing the pins as you go.

4. Attach the invisible zipper foot to your machine and, starting with the right side of your garment, insert the top of the zip's teeth in the right groove of the foot so that your needle falls to the left of the teeth. It is important to have the needle as close to the teeth coil as possible while ensuring you don't sew into the coil. Backstitch at the top and continue sewing all the way up to the mark.

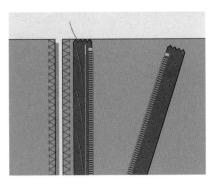

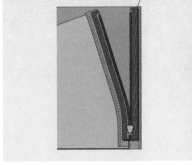

5. Backstitch right on the mark when you reach the end.

6. Repeat steps 4 and 5 on the left side. Take the left side of your garment and position the zip's teeth in the left groove of the foot with the needle to the right of the coil this time. Backstitch at the start and then stitch down until you reach the mark. Backstitch on the mark. Take out your basting to free the bottom of the zip tape.

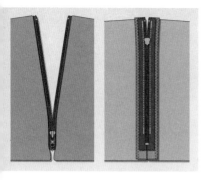

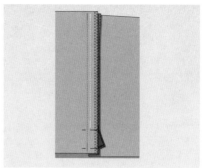

7. Your garment will now be looking like this (from front and back).

8. Close your zip and pin along the back seam with right sides of fabric together. Pin closed the open section below the zip with the right sides of the fabric together, ensuring the tail of the tape is not caught.

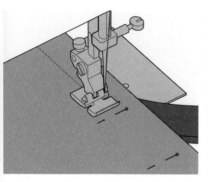

9. Replace your invisible zipper foot with the regular zipper foot (here it is attached to the right side of the bar of the foot). Using a 1.5cm (⅝ in) seam allowance, sew from the zip's seam to the end of your hem. Be careful not to catch the ends of the zip tape, so pull this away when you start so you are only sewing the seam allowance of your fabric below the zip. Make sure you backstitch at the start and end of your sewing.

10. Your invisible zip is now sewn in, you just need to give it a good press to iron it flat. Be careful not to use a too-hot iron as that may damage/curl a plastic zip coil.

Fabric
& Patterns

Selvedge

The selvedge (derived from self-edge) is the finished edge of a piece of fabric, which stops it from unravelling and fraying. It is found on both sides of the fabric, along the length on woven and flat-knitted fabrics and as a narrow border running lengthways along the whole fabric (not the cut edge). It is generally a little different to the main body of the fabric – usually thicker and stronger – and sometimes has the fabric manufacturer's details on it.

The selvedge can vary in width, but most are around 1.5cm (⅝ in) wide. You will often see perforated holes along the edge, where the fabric was held on the loom during manufacture.

It is important to understand what the selvedge is as it helps garment makers to identify the fabric grain or warp direction (see Grainline, page 76) in order to cut pattern pieces correctly. The selvedge is parallel to the warp yarns of the woven fabric structure, and most patterns are usually laid parallel to the selvedge.

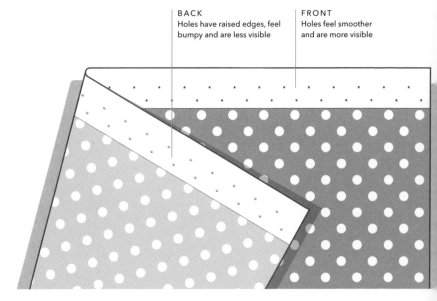

BACK
Holes have raised edges, feel bumpy and are less visible

FRONT
Holes feel smoother and are more visible

Washing & Ironing

It is highly recommended that you wash and dry fabric before sewing to avoid your finished project shrinking. Ironing and pressing are also an important part of the making process – they are your sewing machine's best friend! Some fabrics have care symbols on the selvedge, otherwise follow the general guidance for different fabric types.

Pre-washing

Most natural materials such as cotton, linen and silk shrink when you wash them. Cotton fabrics shrink an average of five per cent but can sometimes be more, so if you don't wash your fabric before sewing and then wash your final garment, it may not fit properly.

Pre-washing fabric also gets rid of any dirt, chemicals and excess dye from the production process. If you are washing your fabric with other things, make sure you wash similar colours together to avoid excess dye in the new fabric from staining. It's a good idea to use a colour catcher for really vibrant and dark colours.

For fabrics that are dry clean only, simply steam or iron (preferably with a press cloth) before sewing and cutting. The steam is another way of helping to pre-shrink fabrics. Synthetic fabrics don't shrink so you may not need to pre-wash, although it's still a good idea to get rid of any dirt.

Ironing and pressing

There is a distinction between these two actions: ironing is sliding the iron back and forth on the fabric to remove wrinkles and creases, while pressing is placing your iron on the fabric on one spot momentarily and then lifting and working your way along the fabric to flatten it.

- Always iron your fabric before cutting, otherwise it can result in inaccurate cuts, leading to fit issues.
- Press your garment throughout the sewing process and not just at the end of the project.
- Press seams and darts open or to one side before you sew over them – it really does makes a difference to the final look of your garment.
- Do not iron or press over pins. Pins with plastic heads can melt, and pins can also leave marks on your fabric.
- Be sure to set your iron to the right temperature for your fabric: too hot and you can damage the fabric; not hot enough and it won't iron properly. Always test on a scrap piece of fabric first if you are unsure.

Some helpful ironing accessories include a tailor's ham (a small, padded pillow that is useful for pressing curved seams/areas); a tabletop sleeve board (a slim ironing board that's helpful for trouser legs and sleeves); and a pressing cloth (a simple cotton or muslin cloth that acts as a shield between the fabric and iron, protecting delicate fabrics from scorching or melting, and preventing shine).

Grainline

Pattern pieces for woven fabrics are marked with a line with arrows: this is called the grainline. When you place the pattern on the fabric, this line should run parallel to the selvedge.

It is important to have the grainline of your patterns running in the right direction, as the further you move 'off grain' the more the fabric can stretch and distort, and the resulting garment will not fit well.

Warp and weft

Woven fabrics have threads running both vertically and horizontally. The threads running parallel with the selvedge are called the warp and are the stronger straight grain. The weft, formed of shorter threads, is perpendicular to the selvedge and is known as the cross grain. Most pattern pieces are cut on the straight grain.

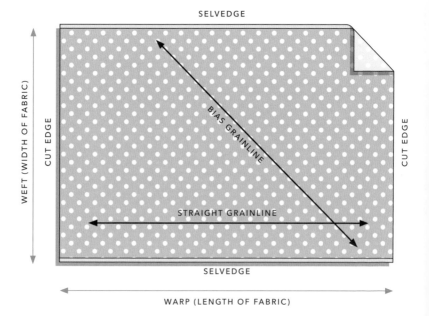

SELVEDGE

WEFT (WIDTH OF FABRIC)

CUT EDGE

CUT EDGE

BIAS GRAINLINE

STRAIGHT GRAINLINE

SELVEDGE

WARP (LENGTH OF FABRIC)

Bias cut

The diagonal of the fabric (a 45-degree angle from the selvedge) is known as the bias. The bias cut of the fabric is stretchy and has more drape. Some patterns are drafted to be cut on the bias, and if this is the case the grainline will be marked accordingly on the pattern and should still be placed parallel to the selvedge.

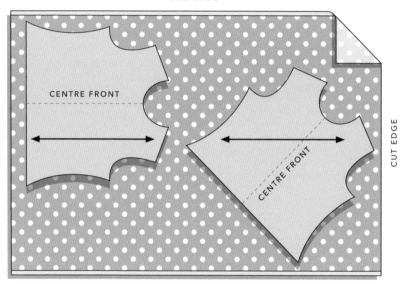

Notches

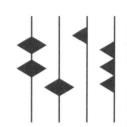

Notches are the U-shaped, dashed, triangular or diamond-shaped symbols that you will find along the cutting lines of pattern pieces. They are there as markers to join two garment sections together, ensuring you are pinning and sewing your seams accurately.

Inward and outward notches

On most commercial paper patterns, both inward (cut a triangle into the fabric) and outward (cut out in a V shape) notches can be found, and you can choose which to do depending on your fabric. For delicate fabrics or those that fray easily it is best to cut your notches outward. For more stable fabrics, rather than cutting the full triangle you can just cut a little snip in the notch.

I would advise you cut notches no deeper than 3mm (⅛ in), especially if your seam allowance is 1cm (⅜ in) or less. It is also important to cut your notch at 90 degrees to your pattern edge.

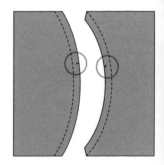

Notches to match seams always at right angles to seam allowance

Multiple notches

When two or more notches are grouped together, make sure you mark the multiple notches. On garment patterns, single notches are usually found on the front garment pieces and double notches are found on the back pattern pieces.

Always double check that you have cut all your notches, as they are really helpful during the sewing process; if you have forgotten them you will need to go back to your pattern to transfer them, which can be a pain.

Mark notches with snips

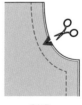

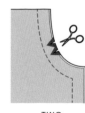

ONE
NOTCH

TWO
NOTCHES

Seam Allowances

Seam allowance (sometimes called inlays) is the distance from the cut edge of fabric to where the sewing machine will sew the seam lines.

Seam allowance measurements vary from 7mm (¼ in) wide to as much as several centimetres. If you're using a commercial sewing pattern, the seam allowances for all parts will be stated. It is important to sew the amount of seam allowance recommended on your pattern instructions, otherwise your make will not be the correct fit. For example, if the seam allowance is stated as 1cm (⅜ in) then you will need to ensure you sew 1cm (⅜ in) in from the raw edge of the fabric.

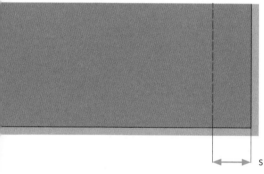

SEAM ALLOWANCE

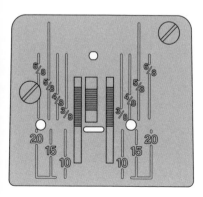

The sewing machine needle plate often has guides where you can align your fabric edge to help you to easily and accurately sew the neccesary seam allowance. If your sewing machine does not have seam allowance guides, try putting masking tape or an elastic band over the bed of your machine and use this as a guide for the edge of your fabric.

Understanding Patterns

Sometimes you'll want to use commercial patterns for sewing projects, so you need to know how to interpret the information found on them. They can appear a bit overwhelming at first, with lots of lines, shapes, text and symbols, but they are pretty logical once broken down.

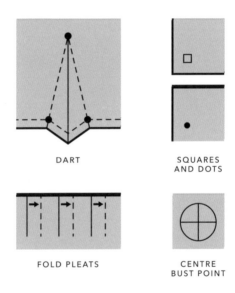

DART

SQUARES AND DOTS

FOLD PLEATS

CENTRE BUST POINT

Centre line: a dashed and dotted line is usually found on garment patterns, which marks the centre front (CF) and centre back (CB).

Darts: these are large, elongated triangles from the bust to the waist, or diamonds from the bust to the hip. Darts are sewn following these marked lines to add shape to a garment.

Crossed circles: these are used to mark the centre of the bust point.

Squares and dots: these little shapes are used as matching points like notches, or can be used to indicate where to start and stop sewing.

LENGTHEN OR SHORTEN LINES

STRAIGHT GRAIN:
PLACE ON FABRIC AN EVEN
DISTANCE FROM SELVEDGE

FOLD GRAIN:
PLACE ON FOLD OF FABRIC

CUTTING LINE

SEAM LINE OR STITCHING LINE

SEAM ALLOWANCE

DIRECTIONAL STITCHING ARROW

CENTRE LINE

NOTCHES

BUTTONHOLE

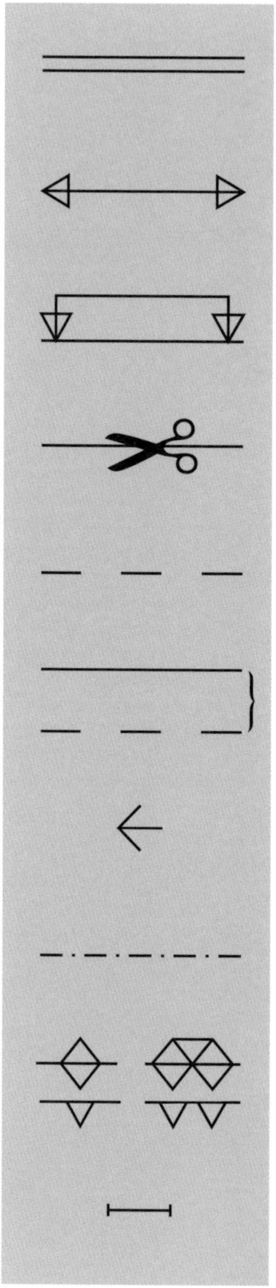

Tip

These symbols are common
across most pattern brands,
but you may occasionally find
different symbols so it's wise to
check the key in your pattern
instructions before proceeding.

Fabric Cutting

Make sure you have an adequate space before you start cutting, ideally a high table (a kitchen island or counter is a good height, rather than a dining table) and a large enough surface area to lay out your fabric. A smooth, solid, hard surface is best. Here are two options for cutting, using scissors and a rotary cutter.

Using scissors

Scissors are the more traditional way to cut. I like using them on most fabrics except delicate silks and stretch jersey, for which I prefer the rotary cutter.

Be sure to adequately pin. I usually pin vertically to the edge of the pattern and within the seam allowance. How many pins you use depends on the type of fabric; for a medium-weight woven cotton I pin roughly between 7–15cm (2¾–6 in) spacing from one pin to the next.

Always use sharp scissors for cutting fabric, sharpening them regularly. Only ever use your fabric scissors for fabrics, as using them on paper will make them blunt.

If you are right-handed, I recommend that you keep the pattern to the right-hand side of your blade. You can use your left hand to hold the fabric you are cutting away. This helps create a little tension and provides more control when cutting. If you are left-handed, do the opposite. But cut the way that feels most comfortable for you.

Try to use the full length of your blade when cutting, and try not to close your scissors at the end but stop short and reopen to carry on with the cut so the flow feels continuous.

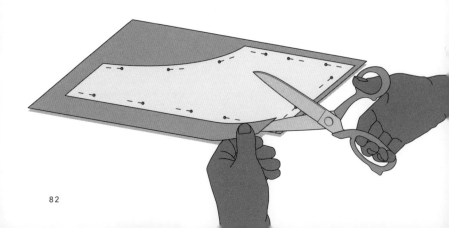

Using a rotary cutter

As well as for cutting delicate and stretch fabrics, the rotary cutter is useful for small, simple square and rectangle-shaped projects like cushions and tote bags. It is essential to use a self-healing cutting mat to protect the surface you are working on. This surface needs to be hard so that when you apply pressure with the rotary cutter it can withstand this.

Make sure you pin down your pattern before cutting. You don't need to use many pins, usually just in the corners of the pattern pieces are enough. Alternatively, you can use small weights to keep your pattern in place and flat.

When using the rotary cutter, ensure you press and lock the blade if your cutter has this feature.

If you are right-handed, it may feel more comfortable to place the pattern on the left of your rotary blade and push the rotary cutter away from you as you work. Do not go back and forth on it, it is best to try to do strong, swift forward strides with your blade.

If you have intricate or small curves to cut, use a smaller rotary cutter or switch to the trusty scissors for these parts. All notches should be cut with scissors, as you will have better control in keeping your notch nips really small.

If your cutting mat is smaller than your pattern pieces, then you will need to move the mat underneath your fabric as you work. Be careful you don't distort your fabric.

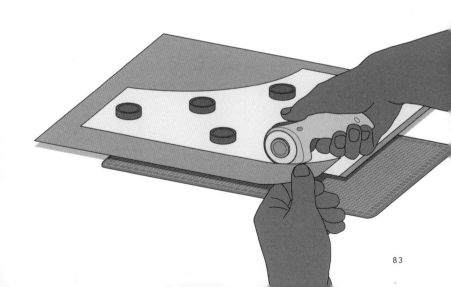

Pinning

It is highly recommended to pin your fabric pieces together carefully before sewing so you have more control while sewing layers of fabric together. You may see different methods of pinning, but I recommend pinning perpendicular (at a 90-degree angle) to the raw edge with the pinheads sitting off the fabric. This way, you can easily remove the pins as you sew, and can stitch very close to the pin before removing it.

PLASTIC HEAD
Sharp, and easy to spot if you drop them; these are a budget alternative to glass head pins

BALL POINT
Designed for knits and jersey, with a slightly different point to avoid damaging fabric

GLASS HEAD
Most widely used, a fine point pin that won't melt if you iron over it

QUILTING
Shorter and finer than other pins, designed to hold multiple layers together

Components to consider

Head: the pinhead, at one end of the pin, can vary in both size and material. Popular materials include glass, plastic and metal. Plastic pinheads can melt under the iron so make sure you use a glass head pin or one with the tiniest metal top if you think you'll be ironing over your pins.

Point: these come in standard, extra sharp and ball point.

Metal: most pins are made from steel but occasionally they can be nickel plated over copper or brass.

Thickness: sewing pins vary in diameter to suit different fabrics. As a rule, use finer pins for fine fabrics and thicker pins for thicker fabrics.

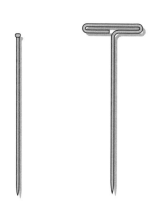

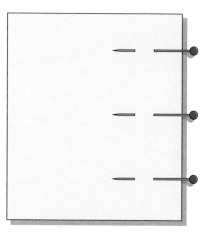

SILK PIN
A fine, sharp pin suited for delicate fabrics

T-PIN
The distinctive shape allows for a strong grip; ideal for heavyweight and bulky fabric

Pins should be placed perpendicular to the needle (horizontal) so that they are easy to remove when sewing

Practice Projects

Tote Bag

This project teaches you how to work with a pattern, cut, pin and sew it. It will allow you to practise straight stitch and using zigzag stitch to reinforce the raw edges, as well as learning to pivot around corners. You can make a flat tote, or be a little more adventurous and add a box corner.

You will need

- 50cm (20 in) cotton canvas, cotton/linen mix, medium-weight denim or heavy cotton
- Matching all-purpose cotton thread
- Tape for the straps: we use 3cm (1¼ in) wide, 79cm (31 in) long (finished length will be 70cm [27½ in]: 4.5cm [1¾ in] is seam allowance at each end)
- Fabric scissors
- Paper scissors
- Paper for pattern (any type)
- Pencil
- Tape measure
- Ruler
- Dressmaking pins
- Tailor's chalk or fabric marker

Tip

If you decide to make a bigger or a smaller tote, consider your strap placement. Pin your paper pattern together to try on one shoulder to see if you are happy with the strap placement first. Remember to mark your notches.

Strap
Cut 1 pair

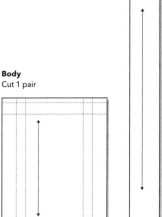

Body
Cut 1 pair

Method

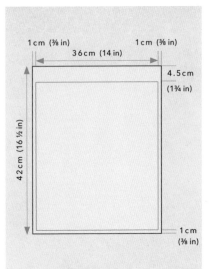

1 cm (⅜ in)   1 cm (⅜ in)

36 cm (14 in)

4.5 cm (1¾ in)

42 cm (16½ in)

1 cm (⅜ in)

1. Create a pattern using a set square or pattern maker ruler. If you have an existing bag that you like the size of, you can use those measurements. Our tote will measure 36 x 42cm (14 x 16½ in). We have added 4.5cm (1¾ in) seam allowance at the top, a 1.5cm (⅝ in) fold, followed by a 3cm (1¼ in) fold. We have then added 1cm (⅜ in) along the sides and bottom.

2. (below) Press your fabric and fold in half, selvedge to selvedge, right sides together. Place your pattern on the wrong side of the fabric, making sure the grainline is parallel to the selvedge. If you are making your own straps, place your strap pattern too, either straight grain or cross-grain. Pin and cut both pieces.

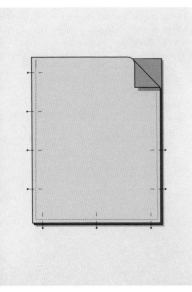

3. With the right sides of the fabric together, pin along the sides and bottom. Sew a 1cm (⅜ in) seam allowance all the way around except the top. Start your seam on the top right side of the bag (remember to backstitch at the beginning). Use a straight stitch of 2.5cm (1 in) length and remember to remove pins as you go. Sew straight down to 1cm (⅜ in) before the corner.

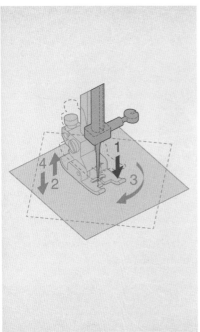

4. At the corner, pivot your fabric 1cm (⅜ in) before the bottom. Remember to lower the needle into the fabric before lifting the foot and pivoting. Carry on sewing along the bottom side of the bag and pivot again at the corner before continuing to sew down the left side. Remember to backstitch at the end.

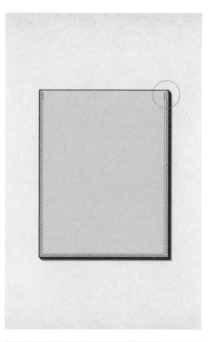

5. Set the machine to zigzag (overcast) stitch according to your machine's manual and zigzag along the stitched sides. Try to ensure the left of the zigzag hits the raw edge of the bag to stop further fraying.

6. Press the side seams towards each other, then fold down at the first notch (1.5cm [⅝ in]) towards the wrong side and press.

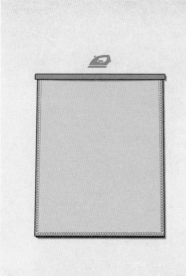

Tip

While ironing, be mindful not to distort or over-stretch your fabric. Gently turn over the fold and press, lift, and then do the next bit, checking the fold to measure accuracy as you go along. Starting in the centre and working out to either end is helpful to retain an equal fold.

7. Fold at the second notch from the top (3cm [1¼ in] fold this time) and press.

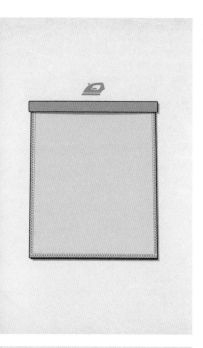

8. Cut your strap tape to length. Unfold one crease at the top of your bag (leaving the other folded) and pin each strap between the notches, making sure the strap ends are lined up with the raw edge of the fold.

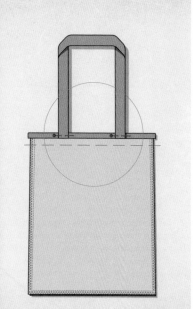

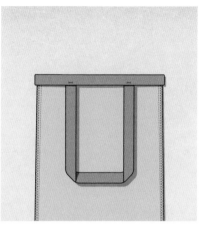

9. Fold the second crease over so the strap now sits on the wrong side of the bag with the ends of the straps sandwiched between the folds.

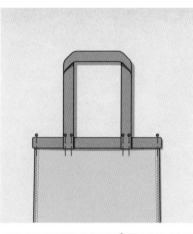

10. Fold the straps upwards away from the body of the tote, and pin the straps down with pins at a right angle. Remove the initial pins in the inside. Place a pin to hold down the side seam allowance of the bag.

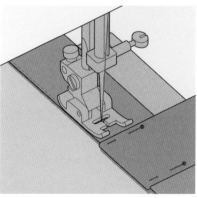

11. Place your bag wrong side facing up and sew a straight stitch between 2-5mm (around ³⁄₁₆ in) from the folded edge all the way around, removing the pins as you go and backstitching at the start and end. If your machine allows, you can move your needle to the right and line up the bottom of the fold with the middle gap of the presser foot as a guide to sew a few millimetres from the fold. Do not take out the pins securing the strap too early; ensure the needle is through all strap and fabric layers first - this will help keep the strap in place.

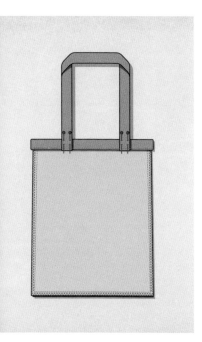

12. Pin the strap close to the top edge of the tote with the pins at a right angle. Place wrong side up, with the needle to the left and the edge of the bag lined up with the middle gap of the foot. Again, don't take out your strap pins too early; wait until the needle is in the strap fabric.

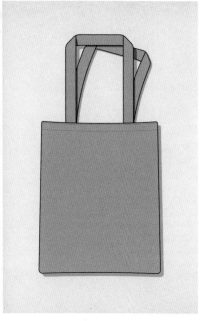

13. Turn your bag right side out and give it a good press. It is now ready as a flat 2D tote bag. If you would prefer a 3D box corner tote bag, please see over the page.

Adding box corners

A box corner will square off the corner of your sewing project, making it 3D. It can be adapted for your tote bag, zip pouch (see page 102) and cushion (see page 118). To sew a box corner, first you need to decide on its size (i.e. what the depth of the bottom of the bag will be). Divide the finished required depth of the bag by two, and that will be the measurement for the box corner.

Method 1

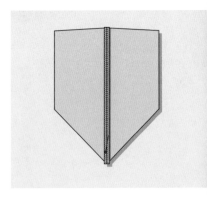

1. Press the side seams open (or to one side if you have overlocked/zigzagged the edges together) and pull the fabric apart at the bottom to make the bottom seam flat and form a point at the end. Check the bottom and side seams accurately match up when pinning.

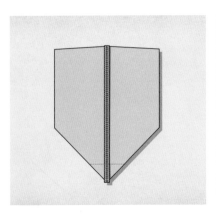

2. Measure from the top of the bag to the depth of the triangle base. Draw a line to mark the size of the base you require for the bag. The longer the measurement from the point of the seam to the baseline, the bigger the box area will be. Sew straight across this line.

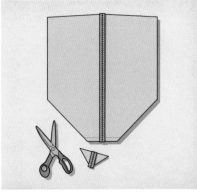

3. Depending on the bulk of the corner, you may want to trim the tip off and neaten the edges with a zigzag or overlock stitch. Repeat steps 1-3 to box the corner of the other side of the bag. Turn your bag to the right side and press the sides and the box.

Method 2

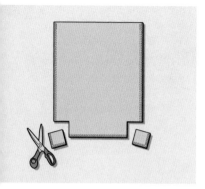

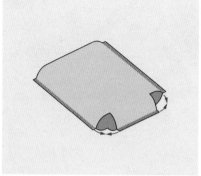

1. Cut a square in the corners to the desired depth before you sew the sides of the bag. It's important to be accurate in the cut width and length to get your desired size of the box.

2. Press open the seams. Pull open the cut edges of the square and match the side seam with the bottom. Pin and sew across the matched edges of the cut corners.

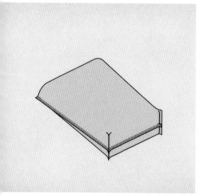

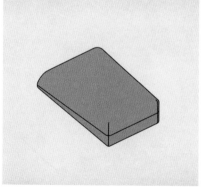

3. Overlock/zigzag stitch the raw edges.

4. Turn the bag the right way out and push out the corners before pressing the bag.

Hair Scrunchie

A scrunchie is essentially a fabric-covered elastic hairband, gathered on the outside with a hidden elastic inside. This is a simple project that allows you to practise sewing a seam, using straight stitch and creating simple gathers with elastic. It can be made in various sizes for a more discreet look or bolder style.

You will need

- Fabric: we have cut a piece 62 x 10cm (24½ x 4 in). You can adapt the size based on how big or gathered you would like your scrunchie
- 8mm (¼ in) wide elastic cut to 22cm (8 in) length
- Safety pin
- Pins
- Thread
- Hand sewing needle
- Scissors
- Ruler/pattern maker
- Chalk or fabric marker

Method

1. Cut your fabric to size (you can cut it on the straight or the cross grain, it doesn't matter). Fold and press 1cm (⅜ in) on one of the short ends towards the wrong side.

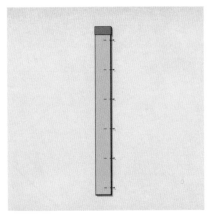

2. Fold over the fabric lengthways, matching the raw edges right sides together, and pin.

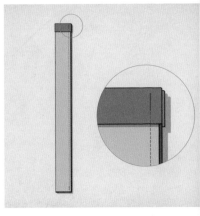

3. Sew a 7mm (¼ in) seam allowance, removing the pins as you go. Remember to backstitch at the start and end of the stitch.

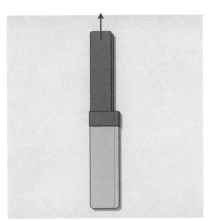

4. Turn the scrunchie right side out. You can do this by attaching a safety pin to the raw end and threading it back through the middle to the other side and out of the opening.

5. Press your scrunchie. Thread the elastic through the fabric tube by pinning one end of the elastic to one end of the tube opening, and placing a safety pin on the other end of the elastic to feed through to the other end of the fabric tube opening. Your fabric will gather on top of the elastic.

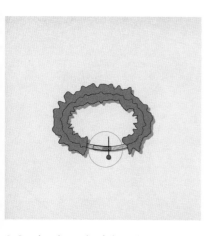

6. Overlap the ends of elastic by 2cm (¾ in). Place a pin and stitch with a zigzag. Or you can just securely tie a knot (this will take up more elastic so you should account for this before cutting your elastic).

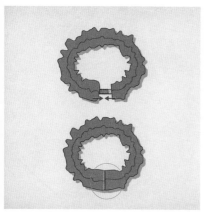

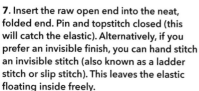

7. Insert the raw open end into the neat, folded end. Pin and topstitch closed (this will catch the elastic). Alternatively, if you prefer an invisible finish, you can hand stitch an invisible stitch (also known as a ladder stitch or slip stitch). This leaves the elastic floating inside freely.

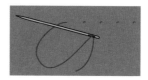

Lined Zip Pouch

A zip pouch is a fun and functional beginner-friendly sewing project. It will teach you how to sew in a zip and add in a lining. It's also a great way to use up leftover scrap fabric, as it doesn't require very big bits of material. And it's the perfect handmade gift.

You will need

- Two 21 x 24cm (8¼ x 9½ in) fabric rectangles. We've opted for a cotton poplin (you can use fusing to make it sturdier) or use a cotton canvas (as we've done with the box corner pouch), a linen cotton, heavyweight cotton or oilcloth fabric rectangles
- Two 21 x 24cm (8¼ x 9½ in) light to medium-weight cotton lining fabric rectangles. Silk is also nice but a little trickier to handle for beginners.
- One 20cm (8 in) regular zip
- Matching all-purpose cotton thread
- 1.5cm wide x 15cm (⅝ x 6 in) length of herringbone tape or ribbon for the straps
- Fabric scissors
- Tape measure or ruler
- Chalk or fabric marker
- Dressmaking pins

Size

The finished pouch will be 21 x 18cm (8¼ x 7 in), using a 20cm (8 in) zip. If you opt for a different length of zip, ensure your fabric rectangles are the width of your zip plus 1.5cm (⅝ in) seam allowance on each side. You can make the length whatever you would like. If you opt for a box corner, this will shorten the bag length so do take this into account. And remember to add your seam allowance!

Tips

The pouch can be easily adapted to your desired size, and you can sew it as a flat pouch or, with a few additional sewing steps, add box corners (see pages 96-97), giving your pouch greater depth.

Method

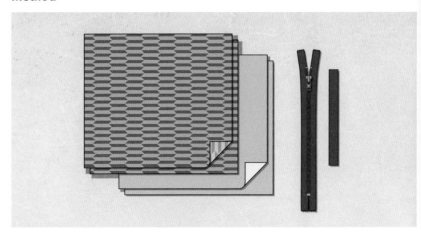

1. Cut your rectangles, 2 x main fabric and 2 x lining. Have your zip and pouch loop ready (12cm [4¾ in] ribbon or tape can be used).

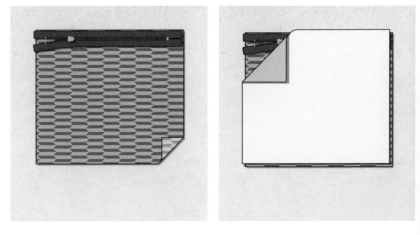

2. Unzip your zip about 5cm (2 in) and place it face down on the right side of the main fabric. If you have a directional patterned fabric ensure that the zip is lined up with the top of the fabric. Make sure your zip is well centred, so both ends of the zip are square with the fabric sides.

3. Place one of the lining rectangles over it with right side facing down so that the zip is sandwiched in between the main fabric rectangle and lining rectangle.

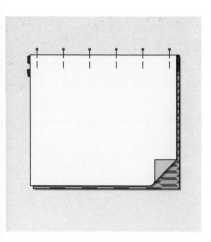

4. Pin all three layers together, ensuring that the top of the fabric, zipper tape and lining top are all aligned nicely. It is helpful to place pins either side of the zip pull.

5. Attach your zipper foot, and sew close to the zip teeth, removing the pins as you go. Remember to pause, keep your needle in the fabric, lift up the zipper foot and pull up your zip, then put your zipper foot down and continue to sew.

This ensures you have a nice straight stitch and not a convex curve around where the pull was. Backstitch at the beginning and the end of the stitching. We have lined up the pinned edge of the fabric layers with the right front edge of the zipper foot, sewing 8mm (¼ in) away from the edge.

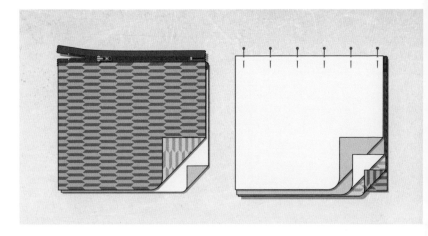

6. Flip the fabric over to expose the other side of the zipper tape. With the zip closed this time, place it face down on the second fabric rectangle at the top (fabric should be right side up). Place your lining fabric right side down so the zip is sandwiched between the main fabric and the lining. Again, ensure all three layers are aligned at the top and are meeting square at the sides. Pin all layers together, making sure all the edges are matching at the top.

7. Sew close to the zip teeth as before. This time, when you reach your zip pull towards the end, keep your needle in, lift up the zipper foot and unzip your pull. Put your zipper foot back down and sew to the end.

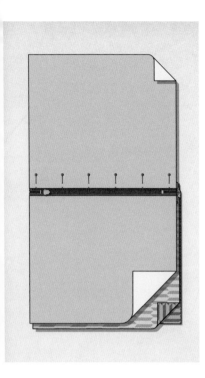

8. To stop the lining of your pouch getting caught between the zip teeth when in use, topstitches holding down either side of the lining are useful. Pin one layer of your lining to the seam allowance on that side (make sure you keep the main fabric out of the way by folding it completely over to the other side).

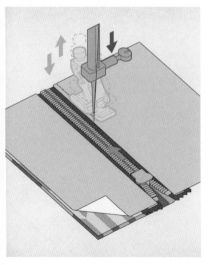

9. Sew a couple of millimetres from the seam of the zipper tape and lining. Move your machine needle to the left and align the seam to the back left of the zipper foot as a guide. You can unzip your pouch to make it easier to bypass the zip pull.

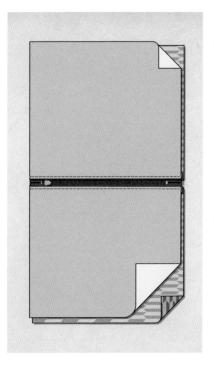

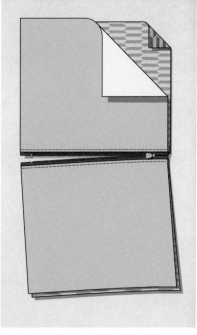

10. Repeat steps 8 and 9 for the other side of the lining to the seam allowance. Remember to only stitch the seam allowance and lining (not the main fabric) in this step.

11. Unzip your zip and then pull the two main fabric rectangles right sides together and the lining rectangles together right sides matching. Ensure the zipper tape matches up at the sides.

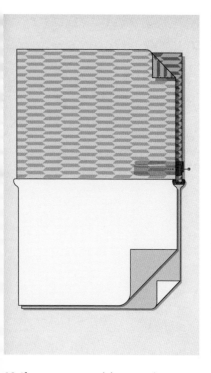

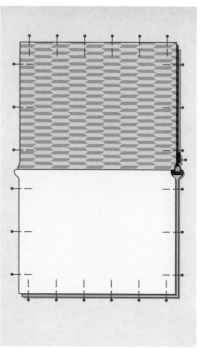

12. If you want a pouch loop or tab, you can insert this sandwiched between the two main fabrics, close towards the top where the zip is open.

13. Pin all the way around.

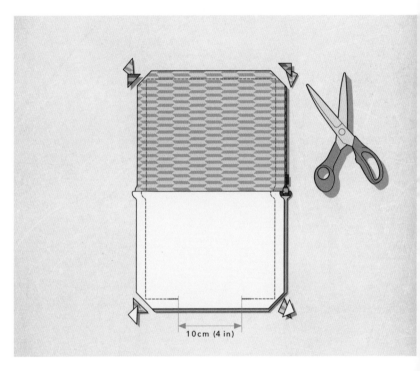

10cm (4 in)

14. Starting a little before the left corner of the bottom edge of the lining, sew a 1.5cm (⅝ in) seam allowance all the way around (pivoting at the corners) until you reach back to the lining bottom, leaving an approximate 10cm (4 in) opening: this gap is to turn your pouch through to the right side. Remember to backstitch at the start and end of your sewing. Clip your corners to ensure pointy corners.

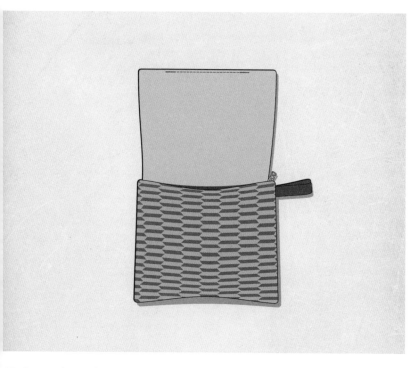

15. If you wish to make your pouch with box corners, see pages 96-97, or for a flat pouch continue to the next step.

16. Pull your pouch through the gap in the lining until you have both the main fabric and lining with right sides out. Pin and topstitch close to the edge to close up this gap: you can line up the edge with the middle gap of the foot and move the needle a few millimetres to the left. Remember to backstitch at the beginning and end. If you prefer not to see a stitch, you can stitch an invisible stitch by hand (see page 101). Push the lining inside, give it a press and voilà! Your pouch is ready for use.

Easy Gathered Waist Skirt

This is a simple garment that does not require a pattern. It will allow you to practise your straight stitch and zigzag stitch and show you how to make a waist channel with elastic running through, creating a lovely, flowing skirt with gathers and a slit to be worn at the back or side. We have opted for a mid-length skirt with a 4cm (1½ in) wide elastic that has a 1.5cm (⅝ in) ruffle on top (the ruffle is optional, you could simply fold over flush to the elastic top edge).

You will need

- 140 x 90cm (55 x 35 in) fabric
- 4cm (1½ in) wide elastic
- Thread
- Chalk or fabric marker
- Ruler/pattern maker
- Fabric scissors

Method

1. Draft your skirt pattern directly onto the fabric. We have used the full width of the fabric to give maximum gathers. If you want a narrower skirt, you can go for much less (anything 20cm [8 in] more than your hip measurement plus seam allowance of 1.5cm [⅝ in] either side).

For the waist channel add 7.5cm (3 in) seam allowance: 4cm (1½ in) for the elastic + 5mm (³⁄₁₆ in) ease + 1.5cm (⅝ in) ruffle at the top (optional) + 1.5cm (⅝ in) seam allowance. Add 1.5cm (⅝ in) seam allowance for the hem.

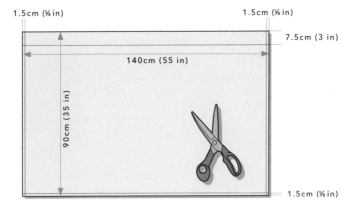

1.5cm (⅝ in)   1.5cm (⅝ in)

7.5cm (3 in)

140cm (55 in)

90cm (35 in)

1.5cm (⅝ in)

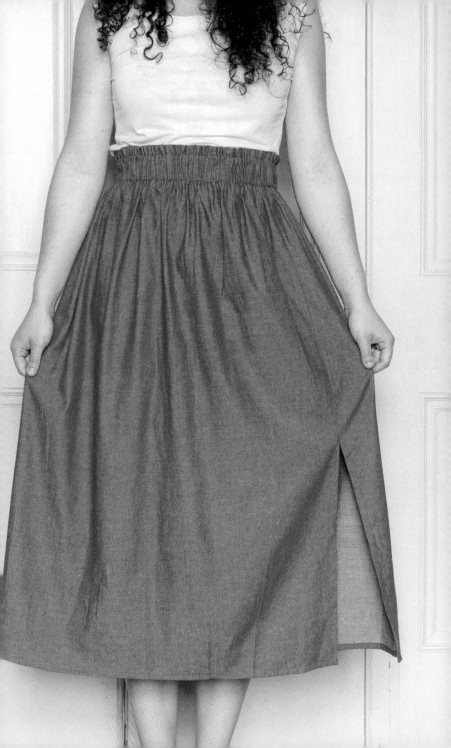

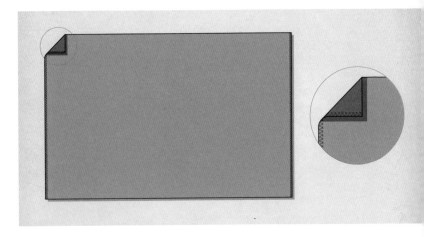

2. Zigzag/overlock the centre-back seam allowance. If you are using the selvedge, then there's no need to zigzag.

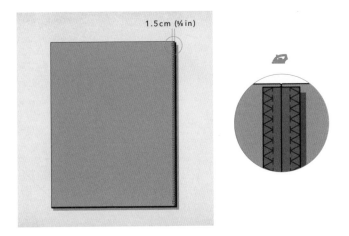

3. Pin the fabric right sides together at the centre back. Straight stitch along the seam, remembering to backstitch at the beginning and end. Press open the seam allowance.

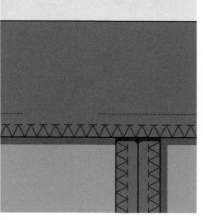

4. Zigzag the top edge of the skirt. Press over 7.5cm (3 in) - or however much you have calculated - of the skirt top over to the wrong side. Pin and topstitch 1.5cm (⅝ in) from the zigzag edge. Leave a 5cm (2 in) opening.

5. If you are including a ruffle, topstitch a parallel line of stitches 1.5cm (⅝ in) from the folded edge.

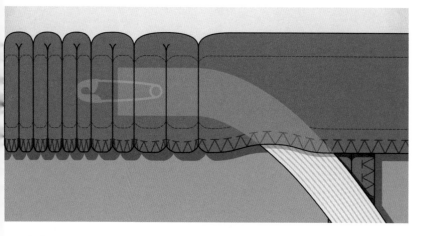

6. Calculate and cut your elastic to length by pulling it around your waist, or measure it to be 10 per cent less than the waist measurement of the intended wearer.

Remember to add an overlap of 3cm (1¼ in). Put a safety pin on one end of the elastic and feed it through the skirt channel opening. The skirt fabric will start to gather.

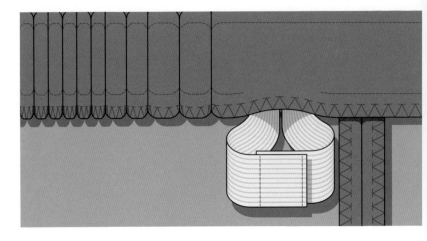

7. When the other end of the elastic comes out, overlap it by 3cm (1¼ in). Pin and stitch it in place with a double line of straight stitch.

8. Push your elastic in and stitch closed. Remember to backstitch at the start and end of this stitch. If you would like to have a slit opening at the back, follow the next step, otherwise skip to hemming (step 10).

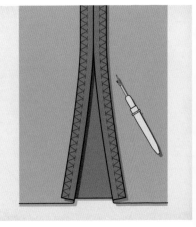

9. Unpick the centre back to however long you would like your slit opening, then backstitch at the slit opening to secure the stitch and stop it unravelling any further.

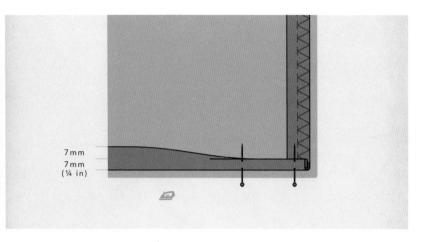

7 mm
7 mm
(¼ in)

10. Hem your skirt by pressing 7mm (¼ in) to the wrong side; fold over another 7mm (¼ in), press and pin.

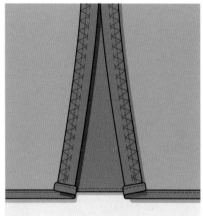

11. Sew close to the edge of the fold. You can line up the folded edge of the hem with the centre gap of your presser foot and move your needle slightly to the right. This is the final step, unless you have opted to include a slit.

12. Stitch a 1cm (⅜ in) topstitch away from the slit opening. Start at the bottom of one side of the slit, cross over at a 90-degree angle at the slit opening and again before sewing down parallel on the other side of the opening. Remember to backstitch at the start and end.

Envelope Cushion Cover

An envelope cushion cover uses just one piece of fabric. It has an opening at the back with an overlap of fabric, which makes it easy to insert and remove your cushion. This project will show you how to draft a simple pattern, cut and prepare it for sewing using the straight stitch, and finish the raw edges with zigzag stitch. You can either add a functional buttonhole and button, or opt for a simple decorative button.

You will need

- 45cm (17¾in) length of fabric, at least 1m (40 in) wide
- Self-covered button or regular button (we used 2.5cm [1 in] diameter here)
- Pins
- Chalk or fabric pen
- Pattern maker/set square/ruler
- Pattern paper
- Pencil
- Needle and thread
- Fabric scissors

Size

The finished cushion measures 40 x 40cm (15¾ x 15¾ in), but you can of course create yours to any size you wish.

Accurate measurements are really important for producing the right size cushion, so it is essential to snip all of your notches without forgetting any. Make sure they aren't too deep, just enough so that you can see them.

Tip

When your cushion is complete, you can 'point out' the corners by gently pushing them out with the tips of embroidery scissors or snips from the inside, before inserting your cushion filling. Also, pinching out the seams with pins while ironing is a great way to get nice crisp edges.

Method

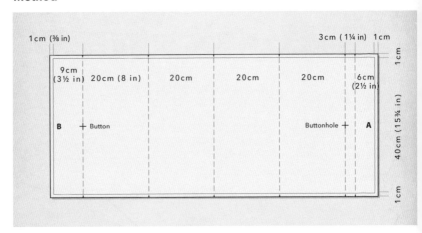

1. Draft your pattern for the cushion. The pattern is in one piece that will envelope to create a cushion with an overlap.

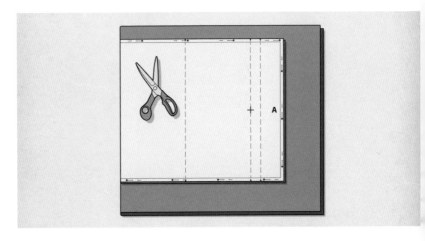

2. Fold your pattern in half and place it on folded fabric that is selvedge to selvedge with wrong sides of the fabric together.

Pin and cut your fabric. Snip your notches, mark button placement on the right side of the fabric, and then remove all pins.

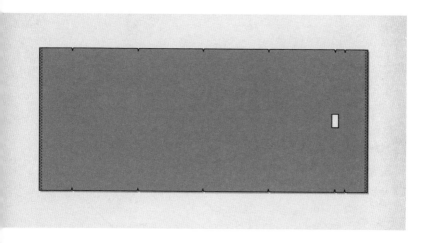

3. Zigzag the raw edge of the shorter sides (side A) of your fabric. If you are adding a functional buttonhole, fuse a small piece of fusible interfacing (4 x 3cm [1½ x 1¼ in])

on the buttonhole marking on the wrong side of the fabric. If you are adding a decorative button, skip this.

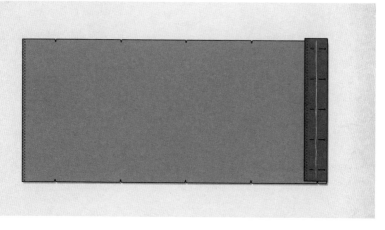

4. With the wrong sides of the fabric facing up, fold over side A at the first notch and press. Draw a line with chalk or a fabric marker down the middle 3cm (1¼ in) from the folded edge; you will see notches matching up at the top and bottom here.

Pin with pins at a right-angle to this line and then sew a straight stitch down it, removing pins as you sew. Backstitching at the start and end is not necessary here.

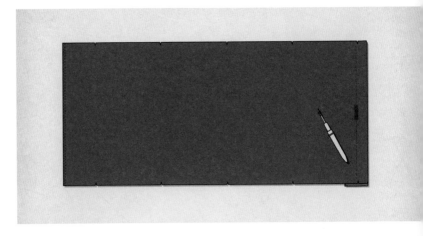

5. If you are adding a decorative button, go to step 6. If you are making a functional buttonhole, turn your fabric to the right side and mark on your button placement according to the size of the button. Now make your buttonhole (see pages 62-63) and cut it open with an unpicker. Practise several on scrap fabric before making your real buttonhole.

6. With fabric facing right side up, fold at the second notch with the right sides of the fabric touching inside.

7. Fold over side B at the second notch. Right sides of the fabric are facing in, touching. Pin along both the raw sides and sew a 1cm (⅜ in) seam allowance. Remember to backstitch at the start and end of each side.

8. Zigzag both raw edges. Secure the start and end of your zigzagging by either tying off knots with the threads or backstitching at the start and end (whichever feels most suitable for your fabric type).

9. Prepare a self-covered button or use a regular button to sew to your cushion cover.

10. Turn your cushion cover right side out. If your button is a functional button, sew this on the underlayer button marking (side B). If your button is a decorative button, then sew onto the top layer (side A). All you need to do now is insert your cushion!

Apron

This is a useful item to make for yourself, or create it as a lovely handmade gift for any cook, baker or crafter in your life. This simple apron allows you to practise pattern drafting as well as adding a patch pocket.

You will need

- Fabric: 1m (40 in)
- Ruler/pattern maker
- Fabric marker
- Paper for pattern and pencil (optional)
- Fabric scissors
- Dressmaking pins
- Herringbone tape (anything from 2–4cm [¾ x 1½ in] wide). You will need 1 x 45cm (⅜ x 18 in) length for the neck strap, and 2 x 85cm (¾ x 33 in) length for the waist straps.

Method

1. First create your pattern. If you have an apron that you already like, you can use that as a template. Alternatively, fold your fabric lengthways and mark your apron as indicated. To create the side curve of the apron, use a dressmaker's ruler/pattern maker, or opt for a straight line from the apron top to the waist.

Draw a 14cm (5½ in) line perpendicular to the fold at the top of the fabric. Move 26cm (10 in) down from that line, and mark 36cm (14 in) perpendicular from the fold. Along the fold, measure 70cm (27½ in) down from the top of the apron. Draw another 36cm (14 in) hemline perpendicular to the fold; connect the side edge of the apron by drawing a line from the two 36cm (14 in) lines. Add a 2cm (¾ in) seam allowance around the bottom hem, sides and top, and 1cm (⅜ in) around the curved edge.

SELVEDGE

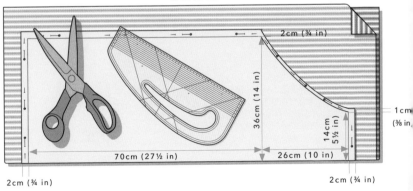

2cm (¾ in)

36cm (14 in)

1cm (⅜ in)

14cm 5½ in)

70cm (27½ in)

26cm (10 in)

2cm (¾ in)

2cm (¾ in)

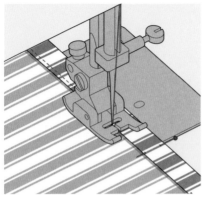

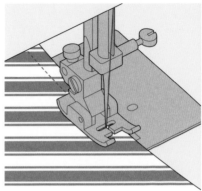

2. As your fabric is doubled, pin it to hold the two layers of fabric together before cutting along your marked outer apron lines. Hem the bottom: double turn up the hem 1cm (⅜ in) and then another 1cm (⅜ in) towards the wrong side. Pin and topstitch a few millimetres from the folded edge.

3. To prepare the curved sides, first stitch a guide stitch 5mm (³⁄₁₆ in) from the edge of the curve. Line up the edge of the curve with the right edge of the presser foot and move the needle all the way to the right.

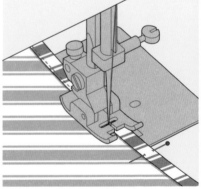

4. Press over the 5mm (³⁄₁₆ in) to the wrong side of the fabric so that the guide stitch is on the edge. Fold over again 5mm (³⁄₁₆ in) and press.

5. Pin in place. Sew 2mm (¹⁄₁₆ in) close to the edge of the fold.

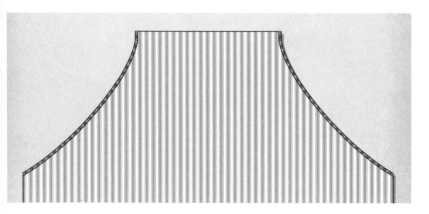

6. Repeat step 3-5 on the other curved side.

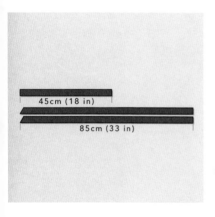

45cm (18 in)

85cm (33 in)

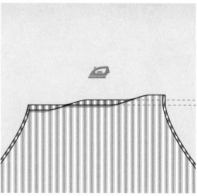

7. Cut your neck strap and waist straps to length. You can decide on the neck strap length by seeing what works best on you. We have opted for a 45cm (18 in) finished length.

8. Press over the top 1cm (⅜ in) and then press again another 1cm (⅜ in) fold.

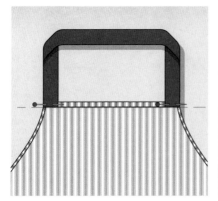

9. Unfold one crease at the top (leaving the other folded) and place the strap ends, making sure they line up with the raw edge of the fold. Ensure your neck strap does not twist when you pin down the other end, as shown above.

10. Fold the second crease over so the strap now sits on the wrong side of the apron.

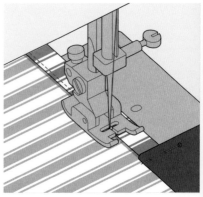

11. Push the straps back upwards so the ends of the straps are sandwiched between the folds. Pin the strap down with pins at a right angle and remove the initial pins in the inside.

12. Sew a straight stitch close to the edge of the folded edge. Remember to backstitch at the beginning and end.

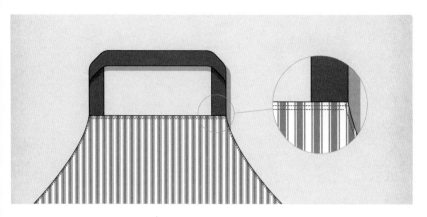

13. To secure the straps further, from the right side topstitch a parallel line of stitches 2mm (¹/₁₆ in) from the top edge.

14. Repeat step 8-13 for the waist strap. For step 13, if you prefer you can just topstitch the strap section and not the whole length down. You can cut the end of the waist strap diagonally to reduce fraying or do a double fold and topstitch. Your apron is now complete. You can leave it as is, or if you'd like to add a handy patch pocket, follow the steps over the page.

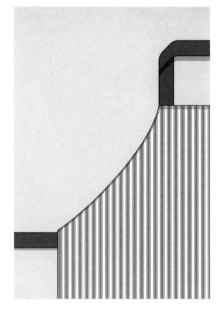

Adding a patch pocket

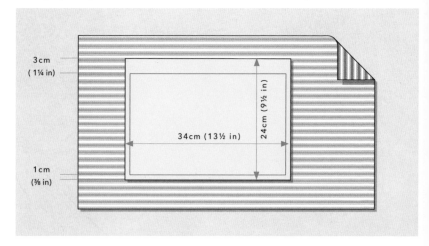

3cm
(1¼ in)

24cm (9½ in)

34cm (13½ in)

1cm
(⅜ in)

15. We have placed our patch pocket so that the top of the pocket is 36cm (14 in) down from the top of the apron. Your pocket can be any size you like, but don't forget to include the seam allowance. This pocket is 32cm wide x 20cm long (12½ x 8 in); 3cm (1¼ in) seam allowance on top and 1cm (⅜ in) seam allowance along the bottom and sides. Cut your patch pocket in the fabric of your choice, on the straight or cross grain. We have cut ours on the cross grain so that the stripes run horizontally.

> **Tip**
>
> You can give your apron a more personal touch by decorating your patch pocket. You could embroider it with your own or the intended recipient's initials, or try adding a fancy trim to make it more unique to you. You could even use a different fabric in a contrasting colour for greater visual impact.

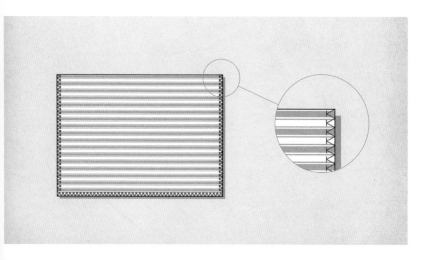

16. Zigzag the two short sides and bottom of your patch pocket to stop the fabric edge fraying. Leave the top raw edged, as this will be turned down later.

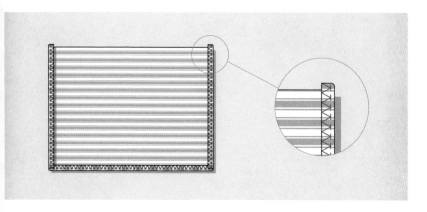

17. Fold the bottom zigzagged edge up 1cm (⅜ in) onto the wrong side of the fabric and then both the sides 1cm (⅜ in) towards the wrong side too.

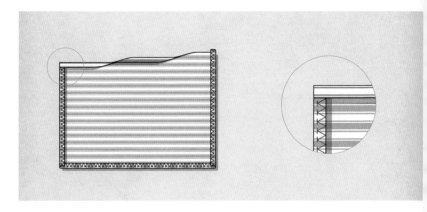

18. Fold the top raw edge over to the wrong side. We have turned it over 1cm (⅜ in), then 2cm (¾ in).

19. Sew this top fold closed by pinning first and then sewing close to the edge of the fold from the right side of your fabric so that it is parallel to the top of the fold.

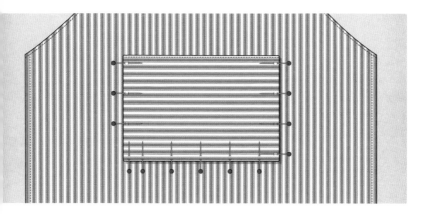

20. Mark the placement of your pocket with chalk, fabric marker or pins. Pin your pocket into place with the right sides facing outward. Pin along the sides and bottom, keeping the top edge of the pocket open.

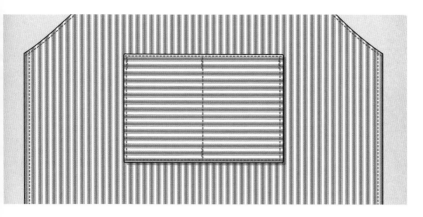

21. Topstitch the pocket in place, starting with the right top corner, along the bottom and then the left side. Centre the edge of the pocket to the middle groove of the presser foot and move the needle to the left a few millimetres. Remember to backstitch at the start and end. If you want to add some fancy topstitching, you can opt for a longer stitch length to look like saddle stitching or do a double row, which will reinforce your pocket for more durability.

22. You can leave your pocket as it is, or divide it into two compartments. Use a ruler/pattern maker to mark a line through the centre of the pocket, and pin to hold the pocket down where it will be sewn. Topstitch along the line, remembering to backstitch at the start and end.

Resources

Be sure to check out the author's own website for tutorials, tips and fun makes: sewitwithlove.com

Sewing machines

babylock.com
berninausa.com
brother.com
elna.com
janome.com
pfaff.com
singer.com

Tools and equipment

UK
johnlewis.com
merchantandmills.com
morplan.com
williamgee.co.uk

USA
americansewingsupply.net
fabricwholesaledirect.com
homesewingdepot.com
joann.com
michaels.com
wawak.com

Brands

Coats threads: coats.com
Gutermann threads:
    consumer.guetermann.com
Pins and needles: prym.com
Scissors: fiskars.com

Patterns

burdastyle.co.uk
butterick.com
madeirausa.com
mccall.com
sewingpatterns.com
voguepatterns.com

About the author

Rehana Begum is the owner and creative director of Sew it with Love. She began sewing at an early age, influenced by her mother's love of the craft, and went on to gain a degree in Fashion Design at London's prestigious Central Saint Martins, where a spell working on Savile Row developed her interest in tailoring and pattern cutting. Rehana has worked in the design departments of several high-end fashion brands including Matthew Williamson, Preen, Margaret Howell, All Saints and Ozwald Boateng, as well as being part of the design team on the TV show *Dancing On Ice*.

Rehana got into teaching when she was offered the opportunity to lead an empowerment project teaching dressmaking to local women in West Africa. When she returned to London she continued teaching at various sewing studios including Sew it with Love, and believes that understanding material choices, clothing and production, and having the skills to upcycle and alter, are more important than ever.

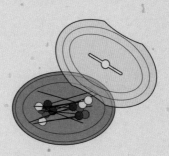

Acknowledgements

Thank you Zara, for offering me the
opportunity to write this book; Akio for
capturing the illustrations with technical
precision and thoughtfulness; Gaynor, our
editor, for your patience, eye for detail, and
for so kindly keeping us in line; Masumi for
putting the layout together beautifully; and
thanks to everyone at Skittledog who has
contributed to this book.

Special thanks to my amma (mother),
Hasibun Nessa Khatun, for teaching me to
sew and instilling a love of creating by hand
from as far back as I can remember. Thank
you to my husband, Rémi, for your love,
support and looking after our daughter Miah
when I started to write this book when our
baby was only six months old. This book has
been my second labour of love. To my family
and friends for proudly championing what
I do, and to the kids in my family, especially
Aya and Isaac, whose excitement for sewing
World Book Day costumes has kept my
machine and hands active. A huge thanks to
my team at Sew it with Love, Danuta, Jeanne,
Brianna and Dilek, for holding the fort at the
studio, teaching our lovely students so I can
focus on writing, and finally a big thanks to
all the students, who have allowed us to
teach you what we love to do!